Praise for *The Care Quotient*

"The key to any successful organization is it's people—their skills, loyalty, their character and dedication to the company. If it's a small business, the people are all—it's make or break. Joseph Gulfo gives the key to caring for and listening to your people in this magnificent book. Skip it at your risk."

—Dan W. Lufkin, Co-Founder, Donaldson Lufkin & Jenrette

"Take the Care Quotient survey to see how much you care about creating the best environment for your employees so that they can flourish and bring your business to new heights."

—Kay Koplovitz, Founder and Former CEO of
USA Network and the *Syfy Channel,* and author of
*Bold Woman, Big Ideas and Been There Run Tha*t

"Nothing that I have read on management... becomes more real world than *The Care Quotient* when it comes to smaller companies which represent 99.7% of employers in the U.S. Building the passion and excitement of a small company is a differentiating advantage. Thousands of people around the world will benefit from this book."

—Fred Hassan, Managing Director, Warburg Pincus and
author of *Reinvent: A Leader's Playbook for Serial Success*

"Small businesses account for 54% of all U.S. sales and 66% of all net new jobs since the 1970's, however, they face a multitude of special challenges often neglected in management and leadership books. *The Care Quotient* provides unique and powerful management techniques for this critical segment of the economy—the engine of innovation and job growth in the U.S."

—Jeffrey B. Kindler, CEO of Centrexion,
Chairman of the GLG Institute, and former CEO of Pfizer

THE CARE QUOTIENT

QUOTIENT

TRANSFORMING BUSINESS
THROUGH PEOPLE

JOSEPH V. GULFO, MD, MBA

A POST HILL PRESS BOOK

THE CARE QUOTIENT
Transforming Business Through People
© 2016 by Joseph V. Gulfo

ISBN: 978-1-61868-793-7
ISBN (eBook): 978-1-61868-794-4

Cover Design by Christian Bentulan

Interior Design and Composition by Greg Johnson/Textbook Perfect

Post Hill Press
275 Madison Avenue, 14th Floor
New York, NY 10016
posthillpress.com

Adele

and to the many others who were patient with me while I tried,

and to Millennials, especially those who I write about in this book—
your inquisitiveness compels me to take nothing for granted;
your WHY's make my BECAUSE's relevant;
your irreverence makes me laugh;
your revelations inspire and validate me;
and your presence in my life makes me a better person.

CONTENTS

Introduction... ix

CHAPTER 1   **Management is a Gift and a Profound Responsibility**..................................... 1

CHAPTER 2   **Reinvent Yourself, as Often as It Takes** 29

CHAPTER 3   **Take the Time to Teach and Mentor, and to Be Taught and Mentored** 54

CHAPTER 4   **Make Difficult Decisions**..........................78

CHAPTER 5   **Set a Great Example**...........................102

CHAPTER 6   **Take Chances on People & Cultivate Talent** 130

CHAPTER 7   **Management & Leadership Tips and Insights**.....................................154

CONCLUSION   **Summary and Care Quotient** 187

Acknowledgments... 205

About the Author 207

What Does Caring in Business Mean?

I was having pizza on August 15, 2015 with my 16-year-old niece, Jennifer, who was trying out for her high school volleyball team. We had just gotten off the beach where I was simulating spikes for her to save by using her arms, shoulders, and pectoral muscles to block the fast-moving ball and keep it alive. She did very well.

I asked how try-outs were proceeding and whether she thought that she would make the team. She told me that her chances were very good and that many of her peers don't quite have the knack. She said that she would like to help some of them by providing tips that were useful to her, but she doesn't want to do so because if they get really good at it, they may become better than she and possibly replace her.

I told her that she should help her potential teammates without worrying about the outcome because sharing knowledge and helping others is always the right thing to do—this is what our faith teaches us, and what Jesus practiced, and so should we. Her father chimed in by saying that the coach will notice and see that you are a leader and a team player and will want you even more. While I agreed wholeheartedly with his point, it bothered me. I did not want

Jennifer to care for personal gain; the moral satisfaction that she would feel deep within should provide sufficient reward.

I then thought about the situation more and made the point that, throughout my career, I actually couldn't think of a single instance in which selflessly caring about a fellow employee, or customer, or investor, or patients did not enhance the business, project, them, or myself, in the long run. And so I realized that selflessly caring not only enhances my chances of being counted among the sheep, as opposed to the goats, but it also is really good for business.

Actually, it is great for business. Selfless caring blinds and numbs you to pain and personal risk; it emboldens you to keep trying—to come up with new solutions, work harder, work smarter, work differently, sacrifice your pride, accept a good idea from wherever it emanates, invite input, and deliver—come what may. Once you behave in a manner in which your personal immediate gain is not your highest priority, the potential for extraordinary results is boundless.

This is the spirit in which this book is written. Selfless caring is not only a great way of life; it also provides for tremendous business success. It is my secret to becoming a manager of very successful companies and projects, and a leader whom many employees I've had the pleasure and privilege of managing would like to work with again.

Selflessly caring in business is my "secular theology."

How did I develop it? I was an altar boy and lector since the age of ten; to this day, when I see a priest celebrating Mass alone, I walk up on the altar and help out in any capacity. To me, Jesus is the greatest manager and leader the world has ever known. I think that the Bible, *The Seven Habits of Highly Effective People* (Steven Covey), and *Crazy Times Call For Crazy Organizations* (Tom Peters) are the best leadership and management books ever written.

The reason that this tome is not in the Religious Studies section of your bookstore is because I don't like turning the other cheek! Not really. Seriously, a business is not church, but it is life—messy, complicated, ugly, and beautiful, all at the same time, and replete with people who are simultaneously damaged in some ways and wonderful in others.

I truly hope that you read this book and elect to selflessly care because in your heart you know it to be the right thing to do, as your mother told you so many times. I also hope that this book will show you how selfless caring is a mission statement, code of conduct, and business policy that will bring great success to those who practice it.

Being a Good Manager and Leader Takes Just One Thing: Selfless Caring

I have worked in start-ups and large corporations for more than twenty-five years and I pride myself on being a manager who truly cares about colleagues. I did not include anecdotes from people talking about their experiences working with me to stroke my ego, but rather to demonstrate the enormous impact that this approach provides. I know that "selfless caring" is a far more effective management style than what many leaders use. I include a lot of details about my experiences—positive and negative—because I know they will be instructive. Some of you may think that I'm patting myself on the back. That's not the point of this book.

Whether you're just starting out in your career or you're an experienced manager, I believe you'll find this book helpful as you focus on "selfless caring." The examples and anecdotes from people working in a variety of fields will show you how relatively small changes in your management style will make a huge difference.

Being an all-star manager is not about dedicating five or ten minutes per day, or following three to ten steps. It is more than platitudes, goals, and aspirations. If you care enough to be the best leader and manager you can be, you will do what I'm discussing in this book naturally, with no checklist required. If you truly care, your customers, company or department, and employees will be on your mind twenty-four hours per day, seven days per week. If they aren't, you don't care enough to be the best, and you will not be.

Managing is a moral responsibility. You literally are responsible for the lives and well-being of those who report to you and those, in turn, who depend on them. The way you make them feel about themselves and the value that you add to their lives will be what they project outwardly to the people with whom they have influence. This multiplier effect is a daunting responsibility. You truly can change the world, one corner at a time, if you care.

Care about what?

Good question. Many business leaders care deeply about themselves—their income, lifestyle, standing in the community, pride, cars, home, and many other externals. Often, these people amass significant wealth; however, they are poor managers and have non-existent leadership skills. But, they care.

However, it is **selfless caring** that is the key to doing the right things at the right time and becoming a highly effective and respected leader. If you selflessly care you will faithfully practice the two most important behaviors that lead to success:

1. Tirelessly prepare by searching high and low for the answer in textbooks, papers, the Internet, and in the heads of experts; and if there is no answer to your exact problem, then
2. Relentlessly trying until something works.

The keys to the latter are having: (a) no pride in objectively determining something you have tried has failed; (b) back-up plans, assuming that the course of action you are attempting will likely need tweaking or may fail; and (c) no fear in reinventing yourself to come up with novel approaches that may work.

Selflessly caring leaders don't hold back; rather they find a way to deliver business results, have their messages resonate, reach employees (even the difficult ones), satisfy customers, and advance their companies.

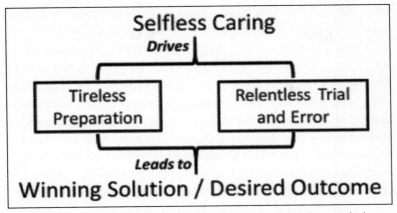

Selfless caring drives tireless preparation and relentless trial and error, which leads to the discovery of the winning solution and desired outcome.

Selfless caring is a character trait that is grounded in a moral belief system whose basic tenets include:

1. Holding principles and truth as your highest order goals
2. Taking personal responsibility for outcomes and results
3. Leaving people and circumstances better than you found them
4. Applying all of the gifts that God, your genotype, and your phenotype have bestowed upon you, even for the most menial of tasks
5. Taking responsibility for the overall well-being of those whom you manage.

Organization of the Book

The book is a collection of anecdotes from my experiences managing numerous people and projects, and running several companies in the biomedical field—biotechnology, pharmaceutical, and medical device. The stories are cataloged under six chapters that represent major themes that flow from selfless caring. The first six chapters answer the questions, "Selflessly care enough to do what?" Along with caring about the right things, they constitute the elements of the "Care Quotient," a tool to evaluate leadership potential and to identify areas of improvement for leaders. Chapter 7 contains specific insights that have been amassed on various topics based on the principles contained in the first six chapters in the form of articles and editorials that I have published. The Conclusion contains a summary of the important lessons of the book, as well as the specifics of the Care Quotient instrument, a management and leadership tool to help identify areas for leadership development.

As part of the research and vetting of the concepts in the book, I contacted several former employees who worked on projects that I managed and in companies that I previously ran. I had not worked directly with any of these individuals for some time, from two to twenty years. Many of them went on to work for other companies and other managers, which brings into sharp contrast the lessons in this book.

The book includes actual narratives that demonstrate the lesson, as well as quotes from former employees about how these actions, performed out of selflessly caring, affected them and motivated them to do the best job possible. In this way, they exceeded their own expectations, which enabled them to develop skills that they never thought they had and positioned them for rewarding and successful careers.

Background

The specifics about many events that are discussed in *The Care Quotient* are analyzed and presented in dramatic living color in my first book, *Innovation Breakdown: How the FDA and Wall Street Cripple Medical Advances.* (See innovationbreakdownbook.com for more information.)

CHAPTER 1

Management is a Gift
and a Profound Responsibility

Having a position of authority relative to others is an honor; it also comes with an implicit promise to enhance the lives of those whom you've been appointed to oversee. Make no mistake, done correctly, it is very hard work; in fact, how often have you heard managers say that the hardest thing to do is to get their work done through other people? The challenging side of managing often obscures the gift and responsibility it represents. The person who selflessly cares enough thinks about this every day, and it often frightens him. The opportunities that a manager has to enhance or diminish employees' lives, and the lives of their dependents, is enormous. A simple smile or compliment on a job well done or a "thank you" can change the mood of an employee, who in turn may treat his or her loved ones in a manner that inspires or encourages them to do something wonderful, and so truly great things can happen for so many because of you.

If you selflessly care enough, you will take this responsibility seriously and tremendous results will follow.

Backdoor Escape

A former colleague, Penny Humphries, who supported me as an administrative assistant at MELA Sciences while she was completing her Speech Pathology degree, told me that she was most taken by how I always gave employees an "out," a gracious way to move on or back down from a circumstance in which they had not performed as required for the good of the project and company. The agreement we had with Penny, who was over-qualified to be working with me as an administrative assistant, was that she would do the work if I made a special effort to include her in business analyses and decisions because she ultimately wanted to run a department or company in her field. It was a two-way street—Penny's insights were very valuable and greatly factored into many decisions that I made.

The fact that she singled-out this behavior speaks volumes to me, because we had many conversations about business, and I included her in virtually everything I was doing; so she saw quite a lot. I firmly believe that when delivering negative feedback to an employee, it is necessary, right up until the moment that the person is no longer an employee, to do so in a manner that preserves his dignity. I think that when pointing-out shortcomings in performance, a manager not only has the opportunity to challenge employees to do better, but also to inspire them to want to be an even greater contributor than is expected. It is more likely that the employee listens, accepts, and changes his behavior for the good of the company if this is done compassionately, and in a manner that not only leaves the dignity of the person intact, but also gives him an opportunity to build upon his self-worth quickly. It is necessary to do this for the psycho-emotional health of the employees; it keeps them motivated and teaches them compassion and empathy, which they will pass on, while, at the same time serving the critical business need. It is an approach that requires knowledge of the person and great touch. You need to deliver the message so that the action is corrected for

2

the moment and doesn't happen again in the future, but you need to leave the person with his pride.

This is difficult to do, especially when you are busy and acting in the heat of the moment, which as CEO of a medical device start-up under great duress from many external forces, was a routine occurrence. Penny had a front row seat to situations like these. Giving a gracious "out" requires a deep knowledge of the person to whom you are delivering the negative feedback, and a focus on the behavior, not the person—hate the sin and love the sinner, so to speak. It also requires empathy and a long view. If you selflessly care, you will take the time to get to know the employees well enough to know how to play moments like these and develop a customized formula for every employee who reports to you.

Perched on a Train

I was once traveling by train with an employee and I was explaining a trick that I use in meetings and presentations. I actually pretend there are two of me—one in the thick of the action (meeting, presentation, debate, or conflict) and a two-inch size me perched with a view of the whole situation. Mini-me is constantly giving feedback about how I am being received, while I then adjust my approach to have maximal impact, or at least to cease doing anything offensive. This discussion took place at the end of the day as we were traveling back to New York from Washington, DC. I made the point that I have been doing this so long that it has become second-nature to me, and that I am doing it right now. This surprised her. I explained that I realize I am the boss and that she is captive and that the last thing I want is to be overbearing and detract from her personal time and invade her personal space. So I said, I am perched right over there (I pointed to the overhead luggage rack across the aisle), looking at whether you are leaning in or pulling back, turning away or anticipating my next word, whether there are any reactions that might suggest I have bad breath, and whether you are feeling good about this or would rather be sleeping. She looked at me quite shocked, as if to say, "Why would you be doing this during a friendly exchange?" and then she said aloud, "Wow, it must be very difficult being you."

Indeed, it is difficult. But, I realized that we are not "friends." Rather as her manager and leader, I had the responsibility to enhance her career. I was doing my job. Selflessly caring managers don't allow themselves to be delusional, that is, to think that employees are their friends. No, every interaction with an employee must be viewed from the perspective of a work relationship and responsibility. This also makes the job very lonely, but, so it is if you want to be an effective leader.

Lending a Helping Hand

In my sophomore high school English class, the American Literature teacher, Br. Anthony Lamb asked us one day, "What is the difference between being kind and being considerate?" No one raised a hand as Br. Anthony searched the room for someone to step-up. Finally, I spoke up making the point that if I were kind, I would give Greg money for lunch if he asked to borrow some; if I were considerate, upon overhearing him earlier telling John that he left his wallet home, I would offer money to him before he even had to ask. "Right," said Br. Lamb, surprised that anyone got the right answer.

Fast forward twenty-five years—an employee got into an accident on the way to work; she was in the middle of a divorce and was living in a small apartment with her two children. She was asking our lawyer whether the company would pay the deductible because she had no money, and she was returning to the office from a work-associated function. The answer was no. Later in the day, I gave her a personal check for more than the deductible. Two years later, I overheard her telling a colleague that her apartment was robbed and her son's school computer was stolen. She was distraught—he absolutely needed the computer for school and couldn't graduate without it. I asked how much a new computer would cost and I gave her a check to pay for it. She was a very proud, independent woman who emigrated to the U.S. from Eastern Europe, and kept her emotions to herself.

I cannot tell you how rewarding it was to see the look of appreciation on her face. I believe that this contributed to her ongoing love of the company. It also established a bond between us, and she felt comfortable giving me honest, and critical feedback on various things like my message(s) at the company meetings or new policies that we implemented. I got back many fold what I gave her, but I didn't do it for that reason, and it is probably why I received such dividends. Employees can detect the intent behind a manager's actions.

Even the Interns

Having summer interns is a great idea for a company, especially a small company, because they are eager, typically high academic achievers, and if you treat them well and they like your company and the staff, you will be successful in recruiting them to the company when they graduate. That wasn't the intent when one of the software engineers asked whether he could have a summer intern to do some routine programming. Then others heard the news and also asked if they could have a summer intern after justifying the need. Poof. We went from a small company of thirty-five employees not really looking to establish a talent-cultivation and acquisition program, to a company with an excellent summer internship program.

I didn't know what was happening until I was told by our HR Director, Vivian, that five interns would be starting the following week, basically one for each department in the company, and one would function as my administrative assistant. I worried that the experience would not be rich enough, that we couldn't provide exposure to a wide enough range of things to make it worthwhile for them. I felt that we shouldn't be doing it because we could not live up to our end of the bargain, and it bothered me, a lot.

So I came up with a plan. The interns would meet as a group for two hours every week with a different department head. The department heads would spend the first hour teaching all of them about the area of discipline in general, as it would be in many different companies, then for the second hour, how that discipline was applied at our company. This would expose them to several different managers and teach them about many different aspects of the company. Also it was an opportunity for our managers, who were young and lacking a great deal of experience, to teach—to organize their thoughts and intelligently and cogently present their departments and their work. This went on for seven weeks. I met with them on the first day for one hour to kick it off and get to know them and explain how the summer would proceed. I also met with them for two hours at the end to explain financing and corporate considerations as the "capstone" session for their summer experience.

It was a resounding success; our HR director presented our program to many universities from which we were able to pick the best and brightest interns for subsequent summers. We kept doing it year after year and wound up hiring some outstanding talent that came to us through the intern program; we attracted superlative performers who would never have come our way had it not been for the summer intern program. In fact, Maceij, one such talent who joined us full time, devised the final algorithm that was selected for use in our FDA-approved melanoma detection device, MelaFind.

This is an excellent example of a small company instituting a phenomenal policy that made tremendous business sense and paid huge dividends. However, it was not borne from explicit research on the topic, best practices sharing, or perceived need; rather it arose from a belief that management is a gift, as well as a profound responsibility because we selflessly cared.

The program was so successful that full-time employees expressed interest in participating. So we ran a similar program after the summer for younger full-time employees, which worked very well to augment their engagement and understanding of the company, *in toto*, and how their contribution fit into the mix. Relationships among employees from different departments formed, which helped create a feeling of connectedness.

Investing in a Person While Selling an Asset

Our company had two products, one of which was on the market but required more optimization. We made the decision to divest this product, called DIFOTI (**D**igital **F**iber **O**ptic **T**rans-Illumination) in order to focus our resources on MelaFind. There was much debate about this, and it did not sit well with the founders and other old timers at the company. I was in my role as President and CEO for about a year when it was apparent that we needed to do this for many reasons. The DIFOTI team leaders promptly left the company; the only person on the small staff that remained was a sales guy in his early twenties named Zack. I didn't know him well, at all, because I was focused on other matters in the company involving MelaFind. Nevertheless, I noticed things about him. He had a solid work ethic, was articulate, and liked by all employees; I could see why he was successful in sales.

Although I did not know the specifics, Zack had a few curveballs thrown his way in life, at which he swung and missed, and he really needed this job, which provided him stability and a home of sorts. Divesting the business was the last thing he needed; here was another curveball, and I felt terrible because I was pitching that day. I wanted to change his luck and his life. He needed a metaphorical hug, a pat on the back, and someone to tell him everything was going to be alright.

So I approached him and offered him a deal; he had very little experience, but he knew the product and customers. I told Zack that if he trusted me and put everything he had into this effort, I would make sure that he had a great deliverable to call his own. I promised that I would spend time with him and show him the ropes. I told him that I was going to have him work with a consultant, an ol' pro from Johnson & Johnson named Jack McGrann who was a business development expert, and with a top deals attorney from a blue chip law firm. Zack did not trust me because he had heard terrible things about me from people who did not agree with my decision to sell the product. I told him that I would make sure he hit this one out of the park and, after doing so he could either stay with the company and work on MelaFind, or leverage the great experience he had gotten into finding a new job.

He reluctantly agreed, but maintained a guarded demeanor around me. I saw the conflict in his face—he was simultaneously interested but also suspicious. I am sure that he was contacted routinely by the individuals who left the company to go work with them, but he did not go. I purposely spent a lot of time with him because he needed direction and a strong influence in his life. The only thing that we had in common was a love for the Jets. So I invited him to a Jets game with my nephews. He showed up, wearing a light jacket, and the temperatures plummeted and snow began falling. I gave him my gloves and a hat. The Patriots killed the Jets. However, we bonded over our disdain for the anemic Jets offense, and the cold weather. Zack began to trust me and to open up.

Jack made Zack put together a list of all the major companies in the sector space and worked with Zack in analyzing their product portfolios to determine whether DIFOTI would be a good fit. They made their list of parties to approach. Under Jack's guidance, Zack developed a pitch, including pro forma income statements and valuation models. He and Jack visited more than twenty-five companies. When things got warm, I would join them. When things got hot, we would then involve our ace lawyer. The effort proceeded for more than a year. I could see the change in Zack—his confidence, depth of knowledge, and comfort in his position. We ultimately reached a deal with a major company in the dental arena. Zack was responsible for the deal, and he was thrilled with himself. I was so happy for him. The company that acquired the product was so impressed with Zack that it asked him to stay employed at our company while its engineers re-developed aspects of the product; and the company subsidized his salary. Zack stayed with us working with the acquirer's product development, market research, and marketing teams; he would pull-in our engineers when needed.

After a couple of years, he received a job offer and approached me asking what he should do; that's how close we had gotten! I told him that he should go because this new company could offer him things immediately that I could not because MelaFind was still in development and had not been approved for marketing by the FDA. So he left and has had a fantastic career, hitting fastballs, sliders, and curves out of the park, regularly. In fact, at the time of the writing of this book, he had gotten accepted into a Harvard Business School program for working professionals.

When I contacted him about this book, this is what he had to say:

> So I am going to do this in a bullet format, note style, and see where it all ends up. I don't know how long I worked with you, but I can tell you that you influenced my career more than anyone before or after you. Here are a few of my memories...

>> I felt you took a chance on me, and believed in me. The belief motivated me to work hard and be successful. I would say I actually worked harder to make you successful, than me. I wanted you to look back on your decisions with me as positive, and that drove me much more than any personal success.

>> You taught me. I remember sitting in your office with your whiteboard and learning how to value a company, which is something that I used at my next company and led to a sale to ____ for ____ dollars. Glad I took notes that day!

You were nice to other people, but not too nice! What I mean here is that you were generally nice to people, which is important to me. If you weren't nice to people, it would have turned me off regardless of your investment in me. However, if someone did not work hard enough in your eyes, or did not perform, you were tough on them. It showed me that when you were good to me, it was because I earned it. I think it's really important for employees to know where they stand with their manager, without needing ESP!

You told me to think for myself. You probably don't remember this, but we were in a meeting with about six people from MELA and maybe four people from ____, and you asked me what I thought about something, and you said "... and don't just tell me what you think I want to hear." Important message, but it was a tough place to hear it. At the time, it was embarrassing, though since then that message has stayed with me. My takeaway was, I have made it this far with my thinking, don't change for someone else, no matter who they are.

You pushed me, but gave me the tools and support needed to be successful. When you came to "EOS" I was a salesperson. Granted, I was a very good one, but I had very little experience outside of that. You put me with Jack and told me to sell DIFOTI. That was an awesome task. You pushed me outside of my standard role, but you gave me Jack, as well as your own time, which were the resources I needed to be successful. Saying you want your employees to grow, but not giving them the resources they need to do so is not quite realistic nor fair.

You provided fair criticism. When I made my first big presentation to ____, you told me before the meeting to pick a theme of the presentation, a message that I wanted them to get, and then kind of stay with it through the presentation. Well, I did just that, except I did too much. When it was over you said, "Great job, but you hit your message too many times, and I think it was overkill. I should have warned you about that." What a great way to give feedback. I don't really know how to sum that up, other than what you read there, but that delivery impacted me far beyond my presentation ability (which is pretty damn awesome right now!).

I have been giving what you said a lot of thought, and looking at my own role as a supervisor, and while I largely agree with your theory of caring about people is enough to make you a good manager, I must add the caveat that you also must convince the people you manage that you do actually care. I have had a few managers that said they cared about me and my success, and very well may have in hindsight, but at the time I was working for them I didn't see/feel it. In order to be a good manager I think you not only have to genuinely care about your people, but they have to see and feel it, and those two things aren't automatically attached. With you, no matter how the criticism was delivered, or what you said, you made me believe that you genuinely cared about my personal and professional success, and ultimately that's why I bought into you. I stayed at the company when _____ and _____ (remember them?!) begged me to leave, but I stayed because I didn't believe you would "hurt" me. I trusted you, and that's not an easy thing to get someone to do. I don't think there's a simple roadmap to building trust, but I do believe it's a critical component of any relationship.

That's it. My two cents at 6 a.m. on a Wednesday. Hope you're well.

My favorite insight from Zack is his first point. He says that what motivated him more than anything was not to disappoint me. What motivated me more than anything was for him to have a successful experience upon which to build his career. Two acts of selfless caring led to an excellent business outcome. Employees want and need to feel a connection with their managers. When that connection is strong, employees are happy, motivated, aligned, and perform their best work.

Zack also raised the point about being tough on people when their performance is not up to expected and demanded standards. Of course, this is important in order to correct behaviors that do not enable good outcomes. But, as Zack stated, it is very important to establish a valid measuring stick. I am a manager who much prefers to manage by positive reinforcement—rewarding and complimenting excellent behaviors. However, without repercussions for poor performance, employees have no guide and true barometer; they can discount the positive reinforcement. I remember early in my career feeling the exact same way that Zack mentioned. An employee was released for poor performance, which was unfortunate for the person, however, it made me feel more valued because it showed me that management can discern a good job from a bad one. I had hope that management actually did notice what I was doing, despite the fact that I received scant feedback.

Don't Ask Others to Do Anything You Wouldn't

When we needed to have our lead product, MelaFind, manufactured according to rigid FDA Quality System Regulation and European Union ISO standards, we elected to partner with a company called Askion, which was located in a small town called Gera in East Germany. Very few people speak English in Gera, but there is considerable electro-optical engineering talent in the region in large part due to the presence of Zeiss, a world-renowned manufacturer of high quality lens systems, in nearby Jena. The whole area was a cold war hotbed of clandestine electro-optical engineering for military purposes. Working with Askion was a huge effort—we asked several employees to relocate to Gera to develop the manufacturing methods, release specifications, release tests, and automated fixtures.

The building that Askion owned was foreboding—four stories, perfectly rectangular, twenty-foot ceilings, long central hallways painted in bright white enamel, and closed doors to every office and engineering suite. Everything and everybody had a place, and when something or someone was out of place, the walls knew it. Although Askion management was very accommodating, the building communicated something very different. So did the cafeteria in a nearby building, which we endearingly called The Communist Café because it had the same menu every day of the week no matter the time of year. If consistency really did make a champion, we were among world class athletes!

On one of my early trips to Askion in June, the weather was very, very warm and humid, and the air did not move. Every window in this humongous building was open to no avail. Notwithstanding the fact that the facility had current, if not state of the art, equipment, it had no air conditioning. There are many things that I can tolerate, but I cannot stand sweating unless I am working out. I was told that working in these conditions is typical in Germany; that their dedication and focus makes it such that they don't even notice it, and that it does not, at all, affect output or quality.

I was also assured that Gera never experiences this kind of extreme heat; that this was an aberration. I did not fall for it. So I asked the President of Askion, Lutz Doms, whether it would be possible to install air conditioning. He provided me a bid to outfit our two dedicated engineering offices and conference room with air conditioning, which we did. I could not in good conscience ask our very smart and gifted engineers and algorithm experts to work in conditions that were dramatically different from the conditions at headquarters. Furthermore, I refused to ask them to do something that I myself would not do.

The systems were a godsend. Our employees were very, very appreciative. Moreover, the Askion employees working on the project were elated. In fact, I was told that many of Askion's best engineers sought to transition to our project because they preferred the working conditions. Every time I visited Askion from May through

October I was thanked by our employees and Askion employees for taking care of them.

The primary reason that I did this was because I cared about our employees and I did not feel that they should have to work in conditions that were unacceptable to me. I did not do it as a means of attracting and retaining the best talent available at the facility, yet that is precisely what happened. The effort was tremendously successful.

Be Present and Available During Bad Times

It is easy and fun to manage and lead when things are going well. I was with a fund manager recently who had previously worked in a big pharma company and then was CEO of a biotech company. He said that the most satisfaction and enjoyment that he has had in his career was when he was running the biotech company and things were going well.

But, things don't always go well, especially in biotech and medtech. In fact, the overwhelming majority of companies actually fail! And, it is precisely when things are not going well that the most is needed from employees. Ironically, however, it is during the very bad times that managers seemingly forget to manage. Actually, I think that they are either so busy, or have such little emotional reserve, that they elect not to manage at those moments.

I have believed since my early days as an associate director of clinical research that very little happening in a company is truly confidential and that if you want untiring commitment from employees, it is best to tell them virtually everything. I remember feeling that I was a pawn or frontline soldier from whom the strategy and changing dynamics of the battle plan were kept hidden. At times, information was hoarded to such an extent, and the leaders were so guarded in their statements, that I questioned the veracity of the information that was shared. I hated that feeling and I vowed that when I became the keeper of the secrets, I would share them widely. Not doing so is simply unfair—employees spend more time at work than they do with their families. This is especially true of tough times. They have earned a right to know what is going on—the unfiltered truth.

Sharing information, however, is not convenient. It requires time, and it creates vulnerability, opening the leader up to criticism, or forcing the leader to think about things that he may not wish to be considering. And, the leader needs to be protected, right? To be in a cocoon as he figures out the best way forward, right?

Wrong!

In this spirit, I made myself available to employees in the bad times even more so than in the good times. I had an office with glass walls and an unrestricted open-door policy. If my door was open and I was not on the phone, any employee could come in to see me, at any time. Seldom did I ever have to say that I could not engage because I was off to a meeting or about to make a call or I was preparing for something. And, even in those circumstances, I at least addressed the issue in some, albeit cursory, fashion until I could re-engage properly.

When MELA was in the deepest and darkest throes of a battle with the FDA and short-sellers on Wall Street, I forced myself to continue this policy. I would also walk the floors, purposely interacting with employees and speaking loudly enough for several to hear when one of them would ask me a question. As a public company in the middle of very difficult times, much was confidential. However, I would tell the employees as much as possible and layout the alternative strategies that were being considered. I would inform them of the outcomes of meetings that I had in Washington. I would also communicate the timetable and my estimate of the likelihood of success, along with any back-up plans that could/would be pursued. When times were bleak, I did not sugar-coat things. I let employees know when there was a chance that we might not prevail. I felt they needed to know that so that they could make decisions about their future and their families.

Doing this took a lot out of me. I was in a very bad way for about a year—sleep deprived, having crying spells, and emotionally at rock bottom. Yet, I always had time for employees with questions, and I would answer them, honestly.

As Vivian Yost, our head of human resources stated in one of her points about the importance of selflessly caring:

Why being honest and having integrity is so important: Being a great leader is about being a great visionary and developing a strategy to get the organization there. However, no matter how great a "visionary" a leader is, if the leader is not able to gain the trust and respect of his people, then the organization will not follow his/her strategy. Joseph was honest with his people, encouraged healthy debate, was willing to admit when he was wrong, and because of that the organization trusted in him and respected him. This was absolutely essential in a "start-up" organization that was growing into a real company. If the leader does not have integrity and honesty, then the people will not "buy into" the vision. Yes, there are always people in the organization that will criticize the CEO, but not once did I ever hear that Joseph was not a man of integrity and good moral values, that tried to do the "right" thing. Even in our darkest hours at MELA with the FDA, Joseph was honest with the organization but showed courage and integrity, which won the most heartfelt respect from the staff.

You cannot have a moral compass, a conscience, or an ability to be selfless without having integrity. Integrity is not something you say that you have; rather it is a way of life that permeates everything you do. Integrity is a character trait that cannot be turned on or off. It is noticed by others, often in difficult circumstances.

As Leela, our director of clinical development pointed out:

Integrity always matters. I wish I could remember the exact situation (and maybe you will and we can jog our memories together). But I remember you sitting in my office and we had just realized some small random caveat that might have a tiny effect on patient care or something like that. I can imagine most people in that position—they would've just dismissed it as being so unlikely as to not matter, let's move, I don't care. We just started thinking about it and then ultimately we realized everything was all good, etc. but I'll never forget how NOTHING ELSE mattered other than doing the RIGHT THING ALWAYS for the PATIENT.

I remember the incident. We were in Leela's office discussing the data from the clinical studies and devising medical arguments in support of using MelaFind. In analyzing the data, I realized that the results from the trial in a certain subset of patients actually proved the opposite point. I looked at Leela and said that not only could we not make the statement that MelaFind can be used in this way, we are actually going to need to educate doctors not to do it. After all that we went through in fighting with the FDA and the public markets, the last thing we needed was to torpedo any aspects of the medical rationale for the product that would be used in marketing. This cut off an important line of validation and medical communication, but, so be it; for the sake of patients, we could not ignore it. We both were very disappointed, but I remember Leela smiling at the end of the conversation, and after reading her comment, above, I now know why she was smiling: she was proud to work here because of our integrity. (Later, when we had the statistician perform a proper analysis on the issue, we realized that we were wrong. We actually were looking at the wrong data set. This was one time where being wrong was a good thing! But, it did not change the fact that our first impulse was to do the right thing.)

As the manager and leader, you are under the microscope at all times. Employees notice everything. They especially notice how you behave under adverse conditions. Because of this, you have the ability to have an impact on people far beyond the existential import of the particular issue at hand. Management truly is a gift and a profound responsibility.

The Golden Rule

Treat others as you want to be treated is one of the most powerful and insightful codes of conduct and themes in life. Indeed, Jesus used this to sum up the "Law and the Prophets." So many things that I did in managing people flowed simply from this teaching, which I learned in first grade. It became second nature to put myself in the position of the employee with whom I was speaking. Following this simple maxim made me a very empathetic manager and taught me to constantly assess how the other party was feeling. How would I know what I would want done or said to me if I didn't know what the other person was feeling? Empathy is a huge part of being an excellent manager and effective leader; you must first understand the other person's state of mind.

When I was COO of Anthra Pharmaceuticals, I developed a habit of speaking to every employee every day, which is possible in a small company. I asked an employee named John who was out of the office for the prior few days how his trip went. He was visiting a couple of clinical study sites in Arizona and Utah. John said, "Fine." I didn't smile, feel great about myself for engaging a "lower level" employee and then leave his work station, rather I engaged him further about the people with whom he met, problems, difficulties, insights from the investigator, and I discussed with him whether he felt that I needed to visit the site. I was not John's direct manager; Denise was. I was confident that Denise would have reviewed all of this and more with John and would bring any significant issues to my attention. This is not why I engaged John, however. I wanted him to know that I cared and I understood what he did in the field, and that I valued his opinion as the man on the ground.

John was very a quiet and serious person, but he perked-up and shared a great deal. In the back and forth, he realized that I actually used to do his job and he appeared to feel great pride in that. A few days later, I approached him and asked him what he was doing. He seemed embarrassed to say as if what he was doing did not warrant my time. He was auditing data that the clinical site entered on the case report forms with source documents (actual patient charts, redacted for confidentiality) from the medical records that they faxed since his trip. I sat down and explained to him how what he was doing was absolutely vital to the business and to our effort. I explained the ramifications of data with "holes in it," the statistical penalties that need to be paid, etc. (In biopharmaceutical and medical device clinical studies, the FDA is predisposed to throwing-out patients from the analyses if the data are not 100% complete. This means that every missing field of information—blood pressure, laboratory results, diagnostic tests, physical examination, patient subjective evaluations at every time point in follow-up, etc. An employee might think that if 90% of the fields are complete, that is acceptable. Not so, *especially* for patients who respond very well to treatment. The FDA scrutinizes these cases the most, and invalidating just one case can mean the difference between hitting the statistical endpoint and not, the difference between drug approval and rejection.)

He beamed. I could see what he was thinking on his face: "Who knew that auditing was so important?" I knew, and I told him. Now he knew, or it was further reinforced. More important, he felt understood and appreciated. And, he did a great job, not just 90%. Explaining the "why" to employees shows them not only that you care to take the time to be with them, but also gives them purpose beyond the specifics of the directions they have been given.

I did that with every employee, including those responsible for the shipping and receiving. Making them understand how what they were doing was vital to the project and showing them how their contribution affects the chances of success, the quality of the product, and the timetable instilled in them pride in their work and elicited great energy and enthusiasm.

I did not do these things to stimulate and energize the workforce or to improve quality and efficiency. No, I did these things because I wished someone did them for me when I was in their positions. I did it because I knew that words from me could make them feel great about themselves, which would last to when they interacted with others, including their families. I did it because I cared. I had plenty of other things to be doing, but this task was important to me. Borne out of selflessly caring, for sure, but the effects from a business perspective were amazing.

Managing Patients and Employees

When I was in medical school and residency, I witnessed people in pain, sick, mentally drained from their experiences, and often paralyzed by anxiety over what might happen next to them. I like dealing with people at their best—no excuses, make it happen, deliver, break down every door! But, patients were at their worst by the time I saw them. I imagined what I would be like in their circumstances—frightened, not medically trained, wanting to believe that I could be helped and that my doctors were the best and also doing their best to help me. I carried these thoughts into every room and every patient encounter.

One day, I was with my senior resident seeing patients and we walked into the room of a sixty-plus-year old woman who was being treated for cancer. It was early in the morning. She gave me a big smile as I walked in the room and took me by the hand over to the window as she said, "Oh, doctor, I am so glad that you came in now; I can show you how I make my macrobiotic shake. I put a half scoop of this, and a full tablespoon from this container, and..." I stood there watching her with a smile on my face, listening to her talk so energetically about what this does and why she adds that. My senior resident came over and said, "Ma'am, I just want to say that research on the macrobiotic diet has shown that it actually does not do much, if anything, to help with cancer, particularly your type of cancer."

Imagine that? This insensitive boor just deflated the spirit of this woman, and studies have shown that patients with elevated moods fair better than those who are depressed. I thought to myself, "And I am the one in training!" I excused myself from the patient and took my senior resident physically by the elbow—he protested because we hadn't examined the patient yet. I squeezed his arm harder and shoved him out the door. In the hall I told him that he was an absolute idiot. Here was a woman, a desperate patient with end-stage cancer who is exhibiting energy and taking control of her disease, and he goes ahead and completely deflates her. He took a deep breath in order to start speaking, so I put my finger up to my mouth in a shush gesture that you would give to a four year-old and then I said, "I don't care if she stood on her head and spit Chiclets; if she felt it was helping her, I would be right next to her on my head, too!"

I went back into the room and asked her to make me a shake and explain its contents. We sat on the edge of her bed and talked, and drank a horribly-tasting concoction of who knows what. She smiled and went on and on about how good it makes her feel. I smiled and nodded and held her hand. Then, I examined her and went on to the next patient.

Sometimes, people—patients, employees, loved ones, spouses, strangers, whomever—just need a little encouragement and someone to be there with them, without rendering judgment. Give them what they need and want in the moment.

Another experience from my residency reinforces the point about how selflessly caring brings with it excellent results; this has to do with clinic duty. When you are a first-year internal medicine resident managing the cases of a dozen to fifteen in-patients with complicated diseases—after an all-nighter with three admissions and a death pronouncement—the last thing you want to do is to go see clinic patients. The primary reason is that their problems pale in comparison to the fires that are burning on the floors. They are also pains in the neck. They don't have their own doctors and they crave attention, so for the least significant things, they want a lot of care while your mind is on all the work you haven't finished on really sick patients on the floors.

Nevertheless, they are people, children of God, and they deserve your best. So I gave it to them. One day, I walked into clinic after the call that I described above and I had fourteen patients waiting to see me, but my colleagues, who were not on call the previous night, only had two and three, respectively. I asked the nurses whether this was right, and they acknowledged that this was the case. So I hopped to it. After seeing six patients and adjusting doses, prescribing antibiotics for throat infections, referring a patient to a cardiologist, and ordering an x-ray on a sore hand, the seventh patient walked-in. He was in his seventies, spry, talkative and eager to talk to me. He asked, "How is it goin' today, doc?" I said that I was feeling well, but I have had better days, but, none of that matters. I am here for you, my friend, I told him. So he told me what was wrong, I listened, felt here and poked there nothing going on. He then said, "Hey doc: you see all them patients out there for you?" I said, "Yes, what's going on today?" He said, "I told them to ask for you because you're the best!"

I thought to myself, "What? Don't do me any favors here! Don't you know that I am exhausted, behind in my work, and I don't get paid a cent more for seeing fourteen patients as opposed to just one patient! In the future, don't do me any favors, you're killing me."

I looked at him and said, "Wow, Mr. ____, that means a lot to me; thank you. Now, about you..." Well, thank God morality is about action not thought!

I constantly carried many oncology patients—the cancer specialists would preferentially admit their patients to me because I cared. I checked laboratory tests, was diligent, and treated the patients with dignity. I also could deal with unfortunate turns of events and death; once, I pronounced three patients dead in one night. In one case, I told the wife of a sixty-year-old man whom I just confirmed had no pulse and was not breathing that her husband had just passed. As I was holding her hand, squatting down by her side, her two sons started fighting, yelling and screaming at first about who loved the father more, then shoving and pulling, so I sprang quickly into action and separated them with both of my hands grabbing their shirts and holding them apart. I began telling them that this is a tough, horrible time and they need to support their mother and get through this together. I turned my attention to the older son, whereupon I saw his eyes widen while looking at his brother, so I turned to see what was happening and was met with a left hook square into my face as the younger brother lunged forward and I held him back—it was clearly meant for his older brother, not my face. I was a bit wobbly, but I didn't let go; by that time, security came in and had the older brother secured and then took control of Joe Lewis. I remember the oncologist coming to see me the next day to apologize; he told me how much the family appreciated what I did. Caring hurts!

I had the privilege of managing the cancer care of many patients whose oncologists were part of the preeminent group in the county. These guys were the best. They practiced by the literature, meaning, whatever the latest paper showed, they did. They were current and cutting edge. I remember having just taken care of a patient with a certain type of leukemia whereupon the hospital admitted another patient with the same cancer. I assumed that we would follow the same regimen. Nope, a new paper had come out in the days between the first patient leaving and the second being admitted, and we changed the treatment plan. I loved learning from these doctors and I was energized working with them, even if the son of an occasional patient slugged me every now and then.

We had just taken care of the woman with leukemia with the new treatment protocol—the course of her care went very well. A week later, another oncologist, Dr. X, admitted a patient with the same leukemia. He called me and told me how he wanted her managed. His strategy was not exactly current with the latest research. So I contacted my favorite oncologist from the other group, Dr. Y,

and asked him if I led the case would he advise me. I was not supposed to be leading anything; rather I was supposed to supporting
and learning from the attending oncologists, since I was an intern, in
my first year of internal medicine training, not an oncologist. Looking back, I don't know how I had the chutzpah to reach out to Dr. Y.
I was only an intern. But I know that there was a better treatment
available for this patient and I had to find a way to provide it, even if
I was risking my position. Dr. Y said he would, but, that Dr. X would
not want him consulting on one of his patients. I assured him that
he would be simply advising me, informally. Again, this is not how
things are supposed to be done, but I wanted to help this woman and
I did not mind taking the risk. Dr. X liked me and had heard about
the case of the previous patient with leukemia, so he agreed with my
proposal to use the new chemo regimen.

Cheryl, the patient with leukemia, was a thirty-six-year-old
woman—her husband stayed at home with their small children
while her mother was at her side every moment. Dr. X introduced
me to them saying that I would be taking care of Cheryl with him.

Managing a patient with cancer is very difficult. Not only must
the treatment plan be enacted, the toxicities and side effects must be
addressed. In those days (1988), the only available chemotherapies
(including the regimen Dr. X wanted to use) were very, very toxic;
the treatments were designed to kill rapidly dividing cells, which
include the cancer, of course, but also non-cancerous cells of the
gastrointestinal tract, bone marrow (red and white blood cells and
platelets), and hair follicles. As the cancer is destroyed, so are many
normal cells. It is a very, very delicate balance, and managing infections and mucosal membrane issues and nausea and vomiting is
tricky and can lead to suboptimal cancer treatment if not done well.
Therefore, I always spent the most time with Cheryl. After seeing
my other patients, I would go into her room with renewed energy
and excitement, talk to her about how she was feeling, fully examine her, check her labs, plan the next cycle of therapy, then secretly

confer with Dr. Y, and finally discuss what I wanted to do next with Dr. X, who also saw Cheryl daily.

Things were going well; she received the first few cycles of the first two drugs of the regimen; we dealt with some toxicities, she was vomiting a lot, but still managed to eat enough. I spent a lot of time with Cheryl and her mom, encouraging her to eat and assuring her that she would tolerate the treatments better with each cycle. Dr. Y advised me, privately; Dr. X was happy. I was feeling good.

A week later, the residency director, I'll call him Dr. King, asked me to be shadowed by three evaluators from the state's medical board—the program was up for re-accreditation. So I had three evaluators on me for a week, watching my every move as I interacted with patients and doctors and staff throughout the hospital, and took ownership of Cheryl's case, which was beyond my responsibility. When Dr. King asked me to be shadowed by the evaluators he told me that the only issue he had with me was that I missed noon conference more than he would like. [Yeah, that's because I was busy taking care of patients, not goofing off!] So he said that I could not miss noon conference this week. OK, I said.

A few days later, I was on call; it was particularly brutal—not a wink of sleep and some complicated patients requiring a lot of tests and case coordination in the morning. By 11:45 a.m., I had not yet seen Cheryl. Dr. X saw me in the hall on the fourth floor heading toward him, which was the direction of Cheryl's room. He asked me what I was doing. I said that I hadn't seen Cheryl yet today. I had the program evaluators with me. Dr. X said that he had just examined Cheryl, that "everything is fine," and that he renewed a few medications for me. So he said, "go to noon conference." I did not like the idea, but what was I to do? So we went. As the elevator opened on the ground floor, I was unable to take a step forward; something inside me literally stopped me from moving. I looked at the evaluators and told them to go down the hall and turn left to enter the auditorium and that I would meet them there before conference finished.

I pushed four on the elevator panel and went back to see Cheryl. She was in isolation because the chemotherapy drugs were working, which meant that she also had very few white blood cells to fight infection. I gowned-up, put on a mask, entered her room, held her hand, asked how she was feeling, and then examined her. Normally, when a patient is in the hospital, you do not perform a complete physical examine every day. You use your stethoscope to listen to the heart, breath sounds, and abdominal digestion sounds, and check temperature, in a cursory and perfunctory fashion. In the case of Cheryl, I performed a complete exam every day; she was MY patient. As I was pushing on the lower right side of her abdomen, she winced. So I moved to the lower left and then back to the lower right; she winced again. I moved to the upper left and then back to the lower right. She winced three out of three times. This was not good at all. Could she have developed appendicitis, or a gall stone, or could she have a diverticulum that perforated?

I ordered a STAT abdominal X-ray at the bedside, and the worst finding that could have been discovered was revealed: she had air under her diaphragm, meaning she perforated her bowel. With a perforation, the contents of her large intestine, which are not sterile, rather loaded with bacteria, are now in her abdomen, and she has no white blood cells to fight the infection. I called Dr. X and the head of the medical and surgical ICU's. The head of the surgical ICU approached me after conferring quickly with his medical counterpart. He said, "Congratulations, doctor, for making this diagnosis, an hour later and she would have been dead. Now, you have a choice to make: give her to me to repair the perforation and there is a ninety-nine percent chance she dies in the operating room, or put her in the medical ICU, give her triple antibiotics, and hope that the perforation heals itself. That has a ninety-five percent chance of killing her." Cheryl's mother started pounding on my chest with both hands, "You killed my daughter!"

[Wait a minute. Didn't you listen to the man? The reason she is alive and even has a shot at all is because of me!]

I grabbed her wrists gently and walked with her over to Cheryl and said, "We need to take you to the ICU immediately and give you antibiotics," which we did. Not only that, when the infection went away and the perforation repaired, we continued the chemotherapy. Ten weeks later, in full remission, I wheeled Cheryl out to her car and helped her into the passenger's seat. She hugged me and we both cried. (The program was re-accredited.)

I didn't care about hospital rules with respect to taking charge of the treatment protocol; I didn't care about getting in trouble for overstepping my authority; I didn't care about getting in trouble for missing noon conference; I didn't care that Cheryl's mother couldn't see what I was doing to help her daughter. At the time, I was doing what I thought and knew was right. Looking back, I understand that I selflessly cared about Cheryl.

A month later, I was approached by the best internist in the county to join his practice when I finished—mind you, I was in my sixth month of a three-year program. When I ultimately decided to leave my residency, Dr. King tried to talk me out of it. He told me that he would let me operate on him after only reading about the surgery the night before! Then, he showed me my file and all of the letters from patients and attending physicians. I had no idea. I still decided to leave hands-on patient care, but I vividly saw how just doing things because I cared mattered, saved lives, and translated into great results.

Selflessly caring made me very well liked, respected, and established. But, I did not do it for that. I did it because that is the attention and behavior that I would want from my doctor if I were a patient. And, as a manager and leader in corporate settings, I behaved in a manner in which I had hoped my managers and leaders had comported themselves when I was under their direction. You see, in the business setting, although you are not dealing with the physical health of people, you have an opportunity to have an equally profound impact on them by augmenting their psycho-emotional health and by better positioning them for long and rewarding careers. And you never know when you will make that impact, so every interaction and situation is important. I looked at this as a moral responsibility. I needed to make everyone under my supervision better off for the experience, while I achieved business success and added value for the shareholders.

CHAPTER 2

Reinvent Yourself, as Often as It Takes

Tom Peters, management guru and author, teaches people how to reinvent companies and ourselves. The first step to reinventing is to recognize and take ownership of the fact that what you are doing or how you are doing it is not working. How does a manager keep himself open to the possibility that what he is doing is not working? Simple, assume that it won't, and don't be wedded to it. That is a major part of the scientific method: test the null hypothesis. Approach whatever you undertake empirically, and you will be open to the possibility that a change is needed.

Care Enough to be Empirical

We like to think that we know everything, or at least everything that really matters, to get the job done. This is especially true of upper level managers and including the President and CEO. After all, we would not have been recruited by power brokers or been hired, if we weren't all that, and more. Right?

Maybe.

Maybe it is the scientist in me, but I never believed that all of the knowledge needed to be a great anything was in books. Of course, you must master the textbook, but in the real world, things are different. If you care, you will do well in school, continue reading and keeping the sword sharp, as Stephen Covey tells us, but if you care enough, you will realize that you are undertaking an experiment. And, as with all experiments, whatever you do starts with a hypothesis, which may be wrong.

What, the boss wrong? Can't be!

Can be, and more often than not, is!

If you care enough, you will approach things with confidence, based on the textbooks that you mastered and your past experience, but you will also realize that even the most mundane activity is actually new and unique territory, and as such, an experiment. You will not be afraid to audit your actions and their effects, and after giving them enough time to have an impact, be critical, and make adjustments or abandon the approach and try another.

Dennis Quinlan, MD

When I was in my third year of medical school in the internal medicine rotation at University Hospital in Newark, N.J., at morning report a resident presented the cases that were admitted to the service from the previous night. Many of the admissions were routine, in fact rote, unfortunately, and the resident mocked the eerily similar cases being presented stating the facts in a sing-song fashion, "Twenty-one-year-old, intravenous drug abuser times five years presents with fever, chills, and coughing...." Everyone sighed and smiled, if not laughed.

Everyone except Dr. Dennis Quinlan, that is. Dr. Quinlan is the smartest doctor that I know, scary smart, in fact. He possessed a subspecialist's knowledge of *every* area of medicine; that's right, he knew more about immunology than an immunologist, more about cardiology than a cardiologist, and more about the workings of a kidney than a nephrologist. He was basically Dr. House, and he ran the Diagnostic Medicine program at the University of Medicine & Dentistry of N.J. (now Rutgers Medical School). I decided to pursue internal medicine because of Dennis Quinlan.

Dr. Quinlan, shall we say, expressed immediate and vehement opposition to the resident's characterization. Basically, he powerfully chided all of us and made the point that nothing is routine in medicine, that there is something nuanced and unique about every patient, even though there were four others with that same exact presentation, and that there is something to be learned in every patient encounter. He didn't even have to say that this was the case for him, as well. No, it was obvious that this is how he approached his craft. And, it is the reason that he was the absolute best, and why he inspired so many.

Dennis Quinlan selflessly cared enough to treat the mundane as unique, and to test himself, every time. Who was I not to follow suit.

The Platinum Rule

My default position is to follow the Golden Rule, as we discussed in Chapter 1. But, what happens when that doesn't work? What happens when you run into people who do not share your background and experiences, so what you would want done to you is not what they would want done to them? You declare that approach null and void, and you come up with a new rule.

You develop the Platinum Rule:

Treat others the way they want to be treated.

This major realization was simply one of many re-inventions of myself that I needed to lead and manage the extremely unique team at MELA Sciences. As the stories below demonstrate, I tried everything I knew to do, and attempted many other approaches. And, I failed a lot. But, I kept trying.

The company was tackling a project that had never been attempted previously: teaching a computer to diagnose melanoma. The founders of the company were in a class by themselves, in every way. I had no shared experiences with them that mattered, other than liking good coffee. They were physical scientists and I was a biological one. I was a "spirit of the law" guy and they were "letter of the law" ultra-precise individuals. They were high-minded and genius intellectuals from the best schools in Eastern Europe and the U.S. I was born in Brooklyn. I was a former seminarian, attending daily Mass when I could, while they had Jewish heritage from persecuted parts of Europe. (One was a Talmudist Rabbi.) I loved sports; they loved Rubik's cubes and 3D chess.

Given the nature of our work—engineering, algorithm development, software development, and medicine—we needed a highly intelligent workforce. We hired the best we could find, and nothing else mattered. We hired seasoned professionals who had just left large companies, and we provided entry-level jobs for newly minted, super-smart college graduates. There were few absolute experience requirements because we were doing something that was truly novel. And what emerged was a highly eclectic group of individuals bound together by a very noble goal—to see to it that no one died of melanoma by helping to catch it early. This goal bridged many a geographical, social, age, gender, religious, and scientific gulf. And it was all that mattered.

Nevertheless, getting things done day to day meant setting objectives, communicating, controlling, optimizing, and doing it again. That is Management 101. For this breakthrough effort, though, we needed to think out of the box, be creative, not be impeded by roadblocks, and look past petty differences. This required leadership, of course, but how do you lead a very eclectic group like the one at MELA Sciences? I quickly learned that "giving a piece of myself" was not the way. My life experiences meant absolutely nothing to Leela, for example, a young hire who was of Indian descent, born in Japan, lived in multiple countries, attended Wesleyan and Barnard, wrote and performed music, and had an alternative lifestyle. She did not know who Rocky was. She was a toddler when *Apollo 13* was in the theaters. She knew nothing of Walt Frazier or Joe Namath, N.Y. sports legends. The same held true, to some degree, for virtually all of the employees.

Management books speak about two types of leadership—the personal (honey) and the positional (vinegar). The former derives from respect and admiration, and comes in time; the latter comes from fear. I needed to lead this group, but it was apparent as I tried many tactics associated with both types that personal leadership was going to take a long time, and positional leadership wasn't going to be very effective. The most gifted of all of them, Dina, for example, nearly quit almost every week for the first several months, usually after a conversation with me. I was more scared of her quitting than she would ever be of being fired.

I also realized that I wouldn't be able to penetrate the circle of trust immediately. Imagine that. By title, I was the leader, right? The CEO. But, that was not the reality. I had to accept that reality if I wanted to be successful. Of course, this was anathema to me; I learned and believed that as a subordinate, I needed to respect at least the office of someone to whom I reported for so long as I received a paycheck from that institution. Not this group. They treated me as an outsider so I decided to stay out of their way, initially. I kept out of their business and instead focused on the two things at which I was an expert while staying at the periphery as the rest of the team focused on the engineering and software development.

Still, I knew that ultimate success required that I get inside the circle eventually, so I carefully observed the group's dynamics. I attended working group meetings during which the esoteric details of optics and algorithm development were discussed in great depth. Because I was unable to judge the scientific merits of the discussions themselves, I chose to spend much of my time observing the behavior of the team. That's when I realized that Dina was a force of nature. At the same time, I decided to bet on the person that Dina herself seemed to hold in highest regard, a young Latvian algorithm developer and programmer named Nikolai Kabelev. Nyq only opened his mouth when he had something intelligent to say, and when he did speak there was little substantive rebuttal to any points he had made.

I began going to Nyq to get the straight scoop on most things. He was excellent with deadlines, and was the kind of person who would work three straight days to deliver on time. I bought Nyq a couch for his office so that he could get at least a few hours of sleep when he went into non-stop work mode. Did he like me? I'm not sure, but he did develop a tolerance for me. Nyq measured people by what they delivered—he used the word often—and when he saw that I delivered too, he seemed to realize that I probably wasn't as bad as their worst fears had made me out to be. We developed a good chemistry. Though I was not an inventor of MelaFind, I joined Nyq and Dina to form the core of the team that took it to the finish line.

But even those relationships weren't easy. With Nyq, for whom I developed "older brother" if not paternal instincts, emotional ties were a no-no. I invited him to my home for a weekend to spend time with my family; we went tubing on a jet boat and he was the focus of my ten-year-old nephew to whom he was a hero. When he delivered on a project with a ridiculously tight time frame, I bought him a geeky watch—a Tissot T-Touch, like I wore—because he seemed very interested in it when I had shown him all of its features (altimeter, alarms, chronograph, barometer, and dual time zone). But, I got him the carbon fiber face, which was much cooler-looking than mine. I could sense that he was developing a trust and warmth toward me.

He must have sensed it, too. One day he said to me, "Joseph, I am from an Eastern European country and I am inherently distrustful of authority." Another day, he said, "You know, it was the nice military officers who you had to worry about." So be it. We would be cordial, but not too much more. Although I was disappointed, I didn't try to fight it, rather I accepted the message. The reality was that he was uncomfortable having a relationship with me.

A few years into my tenure, Nyq and Dina stopped seeing eye-to-eye. This happens in all small companies, and a manager needs to handle the situation. My first problem, though, was that I didn't completely understand the technical details of either of their jobs, so I had no basis upon which to make decisions about who was right and who was wrong. All I knew was that the "secret sauce" (Dina) and the "key ingredient" (Nyq) were not mixing well—for eighteen long months they only communicated with each other through me. And I couldn't order them to work together in the way a manager can when employees are easily replaceable because my threat would have had no teeth. They both knew that I couldn't replace either of them at that critical juncture. So I just kept on reminding them that the three of us needed to get along and deliver the project.

Interestingly enough, I now know that I could have actually ordered Nyq to do whatever I wanted him to do. One day, when I once again brought up a slide presentation with which I'd been urging him to help me, only to be continually rebuffed, he looked at me and said, "You realize that if you simply tell me to do something, I will give you what you want." I realized then that Nyq wanted to be treated like a soldier, and he wanted me to be a strong and confident General. So I began doing just that. The results were golden, I mean platinum.

Seriously, this became my Flux Capacitor (the critical component that permitted time travel in *Back to the Future*, discovered by Dr. Emmet Brown after falling and hitting his head on the toilet bowl). I never wanted to be told what to do, rather I wanted my manager to tell me about the project and the critical elements, and then I would go off and make it happen. I never responded well to being given orders so I assumed that these smart, gifted, self-starters would want to be treated the same way. I would tell them what was needed and why, then get out of their way and wait for them to surprise and delight me. Wrong! Some smart, gifted, self-starters respond to this, and others do not. As the manager and leader, I finally realized that I needed to know how each of the people whom I was managing wanted to be managed—that is, in what circumstances do they most thrive. The question I needed to ask was, "What resonates with them," not "What resonated with me when I was in their shoes?" This is one of the many trial and error, empirical attempts that I made because I selflessly cared. I did not try to force my view of the world, the Golden Rule, which was engrained in me at home and in church all my life. When I saw that it did not work, I tried something else. And if that didn't work, I would have tried something else.

But, it did work.

This was a huge eureka moment for me. I reinvented my approach to management based on it. In so doing, I learned a very important lesson—this is not just for people who appear to be different than I am, rather this is for *everyone*. As I have matured and reflected on my experiences, I have come to realize that every person is different, profoundly different. It isn't fair to employees to not see them as unique. We don't know the micro-experiences that shape the people around us; we were not in their shoes, so we don't know how events in their lives shaped their points of view and inclinations. Consider siblings who are raised in the same house, but can be completely different. Working with the eclectic group at MELA did not teach me to look for common ground with people who on the surface appear to be dramatically different than I, rather it taught me to assume that everyone is unique and to *discover* every employee and customize my approach to them. This was the most profound re-invention of myself that I have ever experienced.

Seeking Help from an Unlikely Source

The manager is supposed to have all of the answers; the manager is supposed to command respect and instill fear just by being in the room. Right? This is the view of the world of many CEOs, and it is reinforced in so many corners of society, particularly in fictional novels, television, and movies. Of course, this is not true. But many people, when they finally arrive at the top, so to speak, believe that it is supposed to be true. So what do they do when they see it isn't? Many become defensive, or try to cover-up their impotence, or exert more positional authority. I did all of that and it did not work. So back to the drawing board, time and time again to try yet another strategy.

In addition to Nyq and Dina, there was one other employee who made an impression on me in those early days. She wasn't an engineer or a physics genius, but all of *those* people nevertheless seemed to like her a lot. This was odd: It was her first job out of college, and she'd been born and raised in the United States, which hardly made her a natural pal for the middle-aged Eastern European geniuses. I'll call her Kathy, and she managed the clinical study sites and organized the interpretation of the pathology slides by our external panel of expert histopathologists around the country. Kathy was clearly very bright, but she also possessed an ability to see the big picture while still catching transcription errors like a transposed set of digits in the fourth and fifth places in a string of eight during auditing. I knew she'd do very well in the highly regulated industry in which we worked.

I asked her to have lunch with me, and she agreed. I ordered a turkey burger and she ordered a salad. I asked her what her goals were, and told her that she had a unique set of skills—big picture and details—that were critical for success in medtech and biotech. I explained to her my problems at MELA, that I simply could not crack into the inner circle and have even a shot of earning a hearing from the founders and other long-time employees. I admitted it to her.

Then, I proposed a deal to Kathy. I would teach her the industry from a clinical and regulatory perspective if she would represent me with the founding group. All I really wanted, I said, was for them to realize that I wasn't so bad. If she could explain that to them—in her own way and in her own time—that would be extremely helpful to me.

While she was mulling it over, Kathy moved a few leaves of her salad, and a roach appeared! But instead of freaking out, she simply moved her plate to the side, looked at me, and said, "You've got a deal." She was completely unflappable! Kathy proved herself an extremely valuable member of our team over time, both in her actual job and in her ability to work well with everyone around her. The latter skill was instrumental in her helping me become accepted by the core team, which was critical.

Admitting vulnerability and weakness is not something you are taught to do in business school. But it worked. Why? I think because it was authentic, just so genuine that it could not be contrived nor invite suspicion. I think it also communicated the major theme of this book: selfless caring. When employees see that you care about the project more than yourself (or people's opinions of you), they care about the project. When they see that you care about them and are going to give them something more than just a paycheck, they care about you and want to help you succeed.

When in Rome...

Managing the team and MELA was the most challenging leadership role that I have ever had. Over the nine and half years, the dynamics of the constituents that needed to be managed changed, as well as the founders, employees, private investors, public investors, vendors, and regulators. In the very early days, I was a fish out of water and I knew it. Nothing felt comfortable or right—I was out of alignment and I needed to bring some semblance of order so that I could wrap my hands around the project. One of the things that I found particularly upsetting was the work hours the early team kept. Basically, there were no "work hours."

I was in the office from 9:10 a.m. to 3:45 p.m. because I had a horrific commute, living in Delaware and working in Irvington, New York, which is in Westchester. From my home in Wilmington, Delaware, the trip entailed a drive to the train station, an Amtrak train ride to Penn Station, one stop on the 1,2,3 line to 42nd Street to connect to the shuttle to Grand Central Station, and finally a Metro North train to Irvington, New York. (The train that I would ultimately take in the morning left Wilmington at 5:20 a.m., so I would lay out my clothes the night before, wake up at 4:45 a.m. shower, shave, leave the house at 5:00 a.m., park the car, get a cup of coffee, and run to the first of four trains I would ride over the next three-and-a-half hours-plus.) And then I would reverse it in the evening, which took thirty minutes longer because the departure times did not align as well as the morning trains. I would save my reading (reports and trade publications) and writing for the seven plus hours per day that I was on the trains. I had a routine; now I needed others to have a routine that jibed.

It was imperative to me that all employees in the early days were available when I was in the office and when I had the need to interact with them, which could be at any time, literally. In the early days, I needed to learn a lot about the people and the project while I was getting my own work done. Just so much can be said in emails, and as the CEO, with the external audience that I needed to satisfy, quickly obtaining the appropriate facts as well as answers to questions that I had, were very important. Also, when questions are not simple, rather highly nuanced and so many things are works in progress, seldom did just one person satisfy as the source. So I would ask Nyq something, which required follow-up with Kathy, who wasn't in yet. When she got in, she would indicate that something changed such that she is no longer in the loop and Nyq was the keeper of the information. So I would go see Nyq, who was there all night and then left the office a half hour earlier. The day would pass and I would not have my answer—it would have to wait for Nyq to check his email, get confused because English was not his first language, give me an accurate reply to a question that I did not ask, and then, finally, be answered the next day when I saw him. You get the problem? And it kept happening time and time again.

I had enough of it. So I mandated a specific four-hour window when everyone needed to be in the office. I also required weekly reports of activities because I was certain that we had mass ineffi-ciencies and a great way of understanding where the problems were happening and how to solve them, and then to prove to the team that I was right, would be to have written records. Well, you would have thought I reinstituted the Spanish Inquisition. One of the found-ers called a board member and complained about my draconian approach and lack of respect for the team as professionals. Seriously? In real companies, people wore suits and ties, not shorts and sandals year-round like some the people at MELA, got in at 8:30 a.m., took lunch at noon, left between five and six p.m., communicated with their peers, and prepared reports. Draconian? Gimme a break!

So I imposed my will and got what I wanted... for a week. Nyq and Kathy came to me and said that they felt that I was making a big mistake; a huge reason why the project was successful was not only the people, but the culture and environment, which was quasi-academic. They told me that the freedom to do their jobs when and how they liked enabled a highly creative environment. If I instituted all my proposed changes, all of that would be gone and the project would suffer.

First of all, I was thrilled that the two of them came to me, that they were not frightened to state their minds, or worse, that they did not act-out in passive-aggressive fashion, instead. Second, I did not like what they were telling me and I believed that they needed to grow up and realize this was a business. But, third, I bit my tongue and asked them what would they do if they were me—how would they herd these cats? They told me to focus on the work product; they said that is what matters, not "face time." As far as reaching people when I had questions, they told me to call them on their mobile phones.

So I did it. I knew that I could always go back to the changes I had transiently implemented. What they wanted took a lot more work from me, but I did it. I selflessly cared enough about the project and them to reinvent myself around the team, rather than demand that they bend around me. As Charles Dickens once wrote, and Leonard Nimoy's Spock repeated, "The needs of the many outweigh the needs of the few, or the one." Too often the leader and manager believes that his needs outweigh the needs of the team, or the company, or the shareholders. Nonsense. This is, again, where selflessness comes into play. Many bosses are egocentric; they believe that they are at the center of universe, however small (team) or large (company and all its stakeholders) the universe may be. The leader who selflessly cares does not possess this view. I knew that the unique contributors, like Dina (who mostly worked from her home), Nyq, and the founders were like artists and needed their studio to be the way they wanted. I needed Kathy to help me with the core team, and she wouldn't be as effective if I did not maintain an environment in which she thrived. In all truth, I became a much better manager for it—focusing on the work, as opposed to the representations of work (time in the office) gave me a great command of the project and better insight into the individuals. It was the right move, arrived at empirically, because I selflessly cared. And, it reinvented my view of the workplace, and how I manage.

Reinventing on the Fly

The term reinventing conjures-up a process, a lengthy and painstaking effort where you literally start at the drawing board. Of course, that is the preferred way to reinvent—first analyze what went wrong with the approach you were pursuing (then salvaging any of the good elements), while challenging yourself and the team to research other solutions and to think of new and outside-the-box ideas in order to craft a potential winning strategy. But sometimes one does not have the luxury to take this time, especially if you are under the gun. It is all the more important that you have made a habit of reinventing as your *modus operandi* for years when in this sort of situation. Also important is having been ultra-prepared so that you can draw on many and varied indexed ideas in your head to apply to the current situation.

I found myself in this position at the single biggest moment of my career—the FDA General and Plastic Surgery Advisory Committee (AdComm) panel meeting at which MELA Science's product, MelaFind was reviewed in November 2010. We were living a nightmare—anything that could have gone wrong did so, and things that can never happen did happen, against us. It was the most desperate situation within which I had ever found myself. We were a publicly traded company that was being unfairly treated by the FDA. Midway through the day at the lunchtime intermission, our melanoma experts told us that the FDA made thirteen fundamental erroneous statements about the disease and the panel did not correct the agency, rather they accepted the statements as points of fact.

I decided to do something out of the ordinary, to reinvent on the fly. Normally, the closing summation at the end of the day would be performed by the person in my shoes because it is an all-encompassing overview of the entire project with emphasis on the most important issues that emerged during the AdComm panel. However, given the nature of the issues, which seemed to be mostly medical, I asked one of our melanoma expert consultants to perform the final summation, which would come following additional deliberations that would be taking place for four hours in the afternoon. This was very atypical. As a precaution, on the chance that the events in the afternoon would necessitate that I would need to make the closing argument, I gave the team a list of the slides that I wanted assembled for me to use later.

Several experts stayed in the war room to help prepare the slides that one of them would use in the summation; several employees (including me) and one of the experts went back upstairs for the afternoon session. We thought things were bad following the FDA's presentation in the morning, however, what happened during the afternoon session was far, far worse. It was surreal watching how the FDA overtly steered the panel toward the negative decision that they wanted, despite the fact that we had done exactly what the FDA told us to do when we met with them at the beginning of the project (we had a binding protocol agreement from the FDA), conducted the largest study ever performed in the disease, and met every endpoint, meaning, the data were above the pre-specified thresholds.

The frustration, disbelief, and anger that I was experiencing transformed me into a state of true shock and resignation to defeat when the vote would come. Leading up to the meeting itself, I was in very bad shape—not sleeping more than two hours per night for several months and having five crying spells per day as we dealt with assault after assault from the FDA and repercussions in the public stock markets, in addition to the normal insane pace required to prepare for the panel meeting. The events of the day, on top of the horrible state I was in, depleted me and left me totally bare. I was calm and very focused in the moment—I attributed this to mental, emotional, and physical exhaustion. I remember feeling my clothes on my skin, or when something or someone would touch me, and I would look at the spot—my hand or arm—or feel my face with my hand when I felt wind from the air conditioning vents. It seemed like my mind was in quicksand and things that I would normally take for granted and not think about, required my full attention to process and comprehend. And everything slowed-down. I knew I was seriously suffering in the moment, but I had to play-out the hand I was dealt.

Yes, the afternoon was a slaughter. I remember only one positive argument for our case resonating with the entire panel—it had to do with MelaFind's performance on lesions of questionable significance. But it wasn't a win on a key, central issue. I knew we were dead when one of the panel members, a dermatologist, said that he had significant concerns about the fact that MelaFind could not be used on 10% of melanomas—those that were not pigmented. That was a blatant error—only 0.7% of melanomas have no pigment. But no one said a word. I wondered whether that was because none of the other seven dermatologists on the panel even knew that to be the case. Or, was it that they didn't care, that the outcome of the meeting was such *a fait accompli* that it simply didn't matter? Either answer portended certain doom for us.

With a half hour remaining before closing arguments, the team came back upstairs and whispered to me that they had the experts' slides ready, that they'd added a bit about pigment-less melanomas, and that the experts were ready and willing to do the closing. But then they also said that they thought the panel simply wouldn't care that fourteen facts that the FDA had presented about the disease were wrong. So everyone actually thought it best if I did the summation. I agreed, and asked the team for my slides. They then told me that they'd decided that two I'd requested weren't necessary, they'd replaced another, and added yet another. I would be getting up to speak literally not knowing what slide would be coming next! But why would the madness have stopped by that point?

One of the experts, Dr. Clay Cockerell then mouthed something to me. I disengaged from the team, took my attention out of the middle of the U-shaped tables around which the panel and FDA were arranged, and squat-walked over to him so as not to be obtrusive. I was open to a good idea from anyone at that point! And Dr. Cockerell is a very, very smart guy. So what pearl was he going to share with me? When I arrived at his chair he said, "I was asking you whether there even needed to be a vote." I understood his point—it was obvious to everyone that it was over. What do I mean by "over?" Well, it wasn't like they were digging the grave. It wasn't like they were lowering our coffin into the grave slowly with rope. It wasn't like they were throwing the dirt back on top of the coffin. No, it was as if the grass on our grave already needed to be cut! That's how dead we were.

I went back to my chair. The team didn't have the other slide that I had asked for in a moment of mental clarity and insight when they returned. I grabbed my notebook. I'd written down the most egregious errors on major points on one page. That page morphed into my notes for the closing summation—things that I *had to remember* to say, aside from the main messages indelibly etched in my brain. I turned to the team and whispered that I knew exactly what I was going to do. I was going to look at each one of the panelists and say, "Shame on you, shame on you, shame on you, and shame on you... you have let the FDA confuse and confound you such that you have been distracted from the main point, which is..." Our counsel's reply: "Don't say 'Shame on you.' Just tell them they took their eye off the ball."

I had two thoughts. The first: nobody ever gets me! Of course I wasn't going to say, "Shame on you!" to the panel members. (I was, however, going to try to make them feel shame at having been duped.) The second thought: I realized that I had never used the expression "taking [one's] eye off the ball" in my life, despite the fact that I love sports—I wasn't crazy about this reinvention!

And then I was called up to the podium by the chair. I had no idea whether the new slide I had asked for was in the deck, just as I had no idea of the order of the slides. I ripped the page out of my notebook, and approached. My main goal, of course, was to win. But I had another goal, which was to get as much as possible into the public record, so as to lay the foundation for a lawsuit against the FDA. (Never say die.) God willing, that wouldn't be needed, but by that point I had to think that way.

What happened next was simply the greatest fifteen minutes of my life.

It was after 5:00 p.m. at that point. And it had been a grueling day of intense emotion. It would all be over soon. On my way up to the podium, I noticed that none of the panelists were focused on me. They were stuffing materials back into their briefcases, collating their paperwork, shutting down their computers, and using their blackberries and telephones. I entertained some scenarios in my mind: this guy was trying to get an earlier flight, this one texting his daughter about where to find the front door key. They didn't care.

I had a conversation with myself, as if the devil were on one shoulder and an angel on the other.

THE DEVIL: *"They're not respecting you, Joe."*

THE ANGEL: *"Don't you think I can see that?"*

THE DEVIL: *"Your usual style of talking fast and rattling off facts ain't gonna work here!"*

THE ANGEL: *"Don't you think I realize that?"*

THE DEVIL: *"So what are you going to do?"*

THE ANGEL: *"Gravitas. Gravitas. I need gravitas."*

THE DEVIL: *"Where are you going to get gravitas, Joe? All the stores are closed."*

THE ANGEL: *"Don't you think I know that?"*

—The devil disappeared.

THE ANGEL: *"Who do you respect the most?"*

JOE GULFO: *"My father!"*

THE ANGEL: *"So be your father."*

So I reinvented, yet again. My father is very formal. He speaks very slowly and deeply. He uses silence as a weapon. And he projects tremendous authority, standing totally upright at all times with a very forceful posture. I got smacked back to reality when the panel chair said, "Dr. Gulfo, you requested five additional minutes, which

I will grant you, beginning now," as his hand came down and struck the timer.

So I did what my father would do. I stood silently until all eyes were on me. The clock was ticking, but I didn't care. The panelists at first looked up, and then just continued with their distracted behaviors. Then they put their bags and phones down and started looking up attentively. Several panel members had actually been friendly and helpful throughout the day. One of them had even stated that the protocol should have been considered the Bible and that we'd followed it chapter and verse. To those panel members, I mouthed, "Thank you," nodded, and gave a small crack of a smile. A couple of recalcitrant members still wouldn't give me their attention. To those two, I did what my father would do. I turned my whole body toward them, leaned forward, and stared at them until they were attentive. The clock was still ticking.

I finally leaned into the microphone, taking a deep breath, and very, very slowly and in a very deep voice said, "Thank you [pause], Mr. Chairman."

I proceeded through a very slow and methodical presentation of the claim (intended use of MelaFind). I started with the binding agreement which, I said, is a *contract*—a *pact*—and that we had lived up to every aspect of our end of that contract. And from that point forth, I simply don't remember anything else I said.

I do remember that not knowing what slide was coming next didn't really matter. Since I was pausing so much, it appeared as though it was by design! When I was finished with the slides, I looked at my single page of notes, quickly scanned them for the most important things that I had to say, and then tried to think of graceful ways to segue between the points.

Some of those segues weren't so graceful. I remember looking directly at the panel member who'd mentioned pigment-less melanomas, and saying, "About pigment-less melanomas, it is *not the case* that ten percent of melanomas are pigment-less. Rather *just*

0.7 percent are pigment-less." I paused, leaned back from the microphone, looked at every panel member, and then back to him, and said "Zero-point-seven percent." I also managed to present data on the performance of MelaFind in children, a question that a pediatric dermatologist on the panel asked the FDA presenter who was unable to answer and left the panel with the impression that MelaFind was not used in children, which was nonsense.

I stated that we had listened with great interest to the conversation regarding use of MelaFind by all physicians, that we understood the panel's concerns, and that we wholeheartedly agreed that those concerns would only be obviated if the claim were limited to dermatologists, and that we would absolutely be willing to do so. I concluded by returning to the protocol agreement and repeating that we had met every endpoint. That we had done everything that we'd said we would do and to which the FDA had agreed. And that we felt we had unequivocally demonstrated the safety and effectiveness of MelaFind. And then I left the podium.

Now, came time for the anonymous voting of the panelists and then public discussion of their rationale.

Another surprise: The automatic voting system would not work. The panel voted on the safety, effectiveness, and benefit/risk of MelaFind for the claim that the FDA had told us to present—as an aid to *physicians* (i.e., not specifically dermatologists) in the evaluation of clinical atypical pigmented skin lesions. And they had to tally the votes by hand. This didn't bother me much because I was totally convinced that we weren't going to win, and by that point I was mentally preparing my comments for the press conference that would take place right after the vote. I was so convinced that we were going to lose that I wasn't really listening to what they were saying. And then I was told that we had just won "safety" by a vote of ten to six. When the first five votes for "effectiveness" were "yes," I started listening again. We won effectiveness eight to six, with two abstentions. But here's where it's all going to come crashing down, I thought, on "benefit/risk."

It was torture watching and waiting for the ballots to be revealed—each positive vote giving me great hope and anticipation, and each negative vote making me feel doomed. It literally came down to the last vote—at that point, there were seven "yes" votes, seven "no" votes, and one abstention. The tension was palpable. Every person in the room was on the edge of their seats. And finally, the last vote was revealed... YES! We'd won!

The FDA official from the Office of Device Evaluation, who'd been high-fiving his peers with each punch landed on us during the afternoon session, was beside himself in disbelief. But our team didn't know how to react, either. I sat there stunned. We did surface a bit of a cheer, but had to settle down quickly because the reviewers had to explain the rationale for their vote.

As luck would have it, the first panelist rattled off some things that concerned her, but then said that if the claim had been limited to dermatologists, she would have voted yes to "benefit/risk." That basically set the template for the remaining reviewers. They explained why they'd voted as they did, and the ones that would have voted YES if the claim had been limited to dermatologists stated so. There was no official tally of these "exceptions," although three panelists said they would have voted yes if the claim had been what we'd proposed from the very beginning of the project (limiting MelaFind's use to dermatologists), and not what the FDA had made us present. That is, benefit/risk would have been eleven votes in favor to just four votes against.

Amazing. We'd won, and even on the claim with which the FDA had tried to sandbag us—a claim and argument that they'd clearly fed to the panel in advance of the meeting to try to effect a negative vote. But they'd failed. The vote was positive! And it would have been even more positive if the claim had been what we'd proposed.

I walked over to the Division Director to ask about next steps. He told me that they would be in touch. Two members of the review team approached me with smiles on their faces, extended their hands, said a heartfelt and sincere congratulations, and then: "We look forward to working with you." They understood the promise of MelaFind and wanted to see it approved.

I asked the dermatologists who had presented with us to accompany me to the press conference. When we got there, the analysts and reporters present wouldn't sit down. A reporter from *Medical Device Daily*, the top trade publication in medical devices, walked up to me and said he was astounded. "I have been doing this for twenty-five years and I have seen a lot of panels," he said, "but I have never seen FDA pre-panel documents as negative and damaging and as openly biased against a product as they were against MelaFind. I have never seen an AdComm meeting at which the FDA blatantly tried to steer panelists toward the outcome they wanted, and I never saw anyone do what you just did." (Another openly pessimistic Internet writer wrote the next morning that we were "back from the grave" and that I was a superhero! So the FDA had shocked even those who had predicted a negative outcome!)

Even when the press conference was officially over, everyone, it felt, needed to speak to me despite the fact that I was numb, emotionally spent, and exhausted. They came one after the other—our investor relations people, our public relations people, our chief financial officer, employees, experts, and reporters. It just kept coming. Meanwhile, employees back at the office kept trying to call me and were emailing me. One of them, a very young engineer named Alexei Smirnov, texted me: "Joe, that was amazing. We were all watching over the Internet." I replied, "Yeah, we did it, feels great, see you and the team real soon." He texted again: "Joe, no, seriously, this was amazing—there are no words to describe it." "Yeah," I replied, "awesome, and now we'll really make it happen." But he wouldn't go away! He texted back, so I had to excuse myself and go off and volley with him a bit (see Chapter 3).

I went back to speaking to those around me and strategizing about the announcement we'd be making the next morning. We had a team dinner, and we tried to deflate, but we couldn't. The excitement was too great. As usual, I slept for only about two-and-a-half hours, then got up, worked out, and headed to a breakfast meeting with our counsel, our IR/PR team, and our CFO. I then took an Amtrak train home. I should have been ecstatic, but I was still numb.

Reinventing Requires an Admission of Failure and Focus

In the example discussed above, if I had not admitted to myself on multiple occasions that our strategy, my strategy, was not working, we would never have been successful. Managers and leaders do not ascend to the top levels by being wrong a lot. Admitting errors is not the path that most books would advise as the way to advancing. But, I believe that to be the case. Many people look to hide the facts when their strategies don't work, or they deflect by blaming others or by citing circumstances outside of their control. I've got news for you: when you are the leader, there is no one else to blame. As my grandfather used to say, "The fish stinks from the head." So take a whiff, and then take a shower, and use deodorant!

Seriously, I believe so much in reinvention as one of the two fundamental paths to being a successful leader and manager (along with its partner, preparation) that we created a core value at MELA Sciences to encourage employees to admit mistakes and rapidly correct them. Would I have preferred perfect and flawless execution? Sure. But, that isn't going to happen with human beings. So we took it head-on and recognized those individuals who rose above the defensiveness and finger-pointing behaviors usually associated with failure by admitting their approach, idea, or execution was not delivering the required outcome, and then did something to rapidly fix it.

Reinventing is not ego-enabling; in fact, it is ego-destructive. Only people who selflessly care can reinvent successfully. I did not care about whether I would be judged a fool if we failed, and I did not think that failing a certain way would be better for me than failing other ways. Rather I took multiple chances, informed by honestly auditing the conditions on the ground, in order to give us the best chance to win, no matter how it made me look or feel. I did not filter the information through the lens of "what is best for Joe" here. If I had, I probably would have had one of the experts whose name is synonymous with melanoma deliver the closing summation. And, we would have lost. I took a chance, not knowing it would work, but knowing that that the other plan would fail. So reinventing requires multiple acts of selflessness—admitting your results are falling short, taking ownership of the reason, and then devising an alternative strategy that may not lead to your glorification. Again, only when the leader or manager selflessly cares is that possible.

"Vision-agers"

What is the difference between a leader and a manager? Much has been written on this topic, but my friend and colleague David Feigenbaum provided the most insightful and useful definition of a leader that I have seen. A leader needs to do everything that a manager does, but, importantly, a leader also must provide a vision around which employees have not yet been organized or motivated. A leader, then, is a Visionager. It is a leader's job to identify a concept, path, direction, course, or strategy that people have not yet accepted, and through force of personality and persuasion obtain their support and alignment. Managers are starting with a group of employees who have subscribed to the vision, and their job is to ensure dutiful execution.

A leader must be able to reinvent himself and the company and then motivate employees to mobilize around the reinvention. I truly believe that in the course of execution there is need and opportunity for managers to exercise leadership skills because even if the broad vision does not change, many adjustments in tactics are made along the way. Excellent managers demonstrate leadership skills in obtaining buy-in to these mini-course corrections. Effective managing is, therefore, a proving ground for leadership.

CHAPTER 3

Take the Time to Teach and Mentor, and to be Taught and Mentored

It is critically important to teach and mentor younger employees, especially in a small company where no one is a pure manager. You need to see yourself in the positions of the younger employees or think back to when you were their age at that stage in your career. It is easy to think that this is just a luxury when there is so much work to be done. But, if you selflessly care, you will make the time to do it, and then stay later to get your work done, if necessary.

Special Situations

I discussed the intern program in Chapter 1. During my first meeting with the group of five interns, I quickly realized that Alexandra would not be challenged enough in her summer assignment as my administrative assistant. I made the point publicly to the group and told her that I would think of some other responsibilities so that the experience would be appropriately enriching for her. Alexandra was, and is, super-intelligent and dedicated. She was only seventeen at the time. I told her that I would give her projects in addition to the administrative work and that she would attend certain meetings and teleconferences with me to see how the business worked.

Her first project was to research the companies in the stock portfolio of a potential institutional investor who would be visiting our offices and to provide me a two or three paragraph write-up on the comparable companies including the analysts' recommendations, recent events that the company announced (including data from clinical trials), and anticipated milestones. I told her that she would then join the CFO, Director of Marketing, and me in the meeting with the potential investor; she was thrilled.

Alex worked for days on the project, asking me questions as she prepared, and providing me with great information that I would use in the meeting. The day for the investor visit arrived, and as he entered our offices, pandemonium struck. One of the managers urgently needed to speak to me, another call from a board member came in, and I was on my cell phone with another investor in the conference room. My mind was not at all focused on the visiting potential investor who Alex brought into the conference room. The CFO, Director of Marketing, and I met with the investor for about thirty minutes when I realized that I had forgotten something in my office. As I was walking to my desk I saw Alex at her desk and I asked her why she was not in the meeting with us. She replied, "Because you didn't come and get me." I told her to join now but she decided not to and drooped her head.

We finished the meeting and I asked Alex to come to my office. I told this young woman that she was very smart and dedicated but that she wouldn't get anywhere until she changed her approach. I told her there are three types of women in business:

- ▶ Wallflowers who go nowhere
- ▶ Women who try to act and talk like men, with whom no one wants to work

55

- ▶ Women who are professional, true to themselves, and are unafraid

I told her she needed to stop being the first and start being the third. I also told her that when the President and CEO tells you to sit next to him in a meeting, wild horses shouldn't stop you from being there and no further invitation is required.

Well, she left my office crying and didn't come into work the next day. She then came back and we talked about what happened some and she ended up having an excellent summer. She even spent a weekend at my home with my family at the beach. At the end of the summer, before she left for school, she made me a piece of pottery with a quote from my idol, Atticus Finch, *"You never really understand a person until you consider things from his point of view... until you climb into his skin and walk around in it."* I cried. She cried.

Alex would come back every summer and then take a part-time job at the company while she attended school. She showed me a paper that she wrote for her Women in Business course, and she told me that she had an argument with a famous professor at the school who told the class that *a priori*, men cannot be feminists. She objected to the teacher, told her about me and wrote a paper about our experiences to prove that I am a feminist. I cried again. She ultimately joined the company full time and was a stellar employee. In fact, the Pre-Market Approval Application to the FDA for our product would not have been filed on time, nor would we have had successful inspections by the FDA and European authorities, without her.

How did this excellent business result come to be? It was not because of some policy that we put in place or with the foresight that cultivating interns would make for fantastic employees. It happened because we selflessly cared about teaching a young person and being a positive influence in her life.

When I contacted Alex about this book, she was eager to meet. We decide to have lunch; she now works in social services for New

York City and her area of focus is LGBT (Lesbian, Gay, Bisexual, and Transgender) issues. When we met in Grand Central, she gave me a big smile and a warm hug hello. During lunch, I gave her a copy of my first book, *Innovation Breakdown, How the FDA & Wall Street Cripple Medical Advances.* She told me that she now reads books exclusively by female authors, but she will make an exception in my case—I reminded her that I have a very active feminine side, which made her laugh. We talked and had a great lunch. As she departed, I asked if she would ever come to work with me again, and she said yes. That response was very gratifying.

Youth is Wonderful

In small companies, talent acquisition is a huge problem. Who wants to come to a development-stage company with little resources, limited funding, and no product on the market? We were competing with profitable companies for talent and therefore we typically attracted older professionals who were tired of working in big companies, or who took an early retirement package but had plenty to offer, as well as young, fresh graduates. We would often team-up the two—a sixty-two-year-old plus a twenty-three-year-old = eighty-five divided by two = a forty-two-and-a-half-year-old. It actually worked out that way—the inquisitiveness and energy of the twenty-somethings guided by the wisdom of the sixty-somethings made for what you would expect from a forty-year-old.

I loved having young employees in the company. I felt a particular sense of responsibility toward them. I felt that we needed to teach them how to work and give them a firm foundation upon which they could establish a career. If our development efforts worked, I would want them to build their careers with us; if not, at least they received a great experience on which to build them elsewhere.

Leela, an extremely gifted and talented young employee (see Chapter 6) shared this with me:

The youth—you love the youth! I attended the premiere of the Meredith Vieira show when it actually aired so I was with the crew and all, and Meredith gave a speech talking to the YOUTH and the interns directly... I mean, it was classic Gulfo! I said that to my friend. I mean you've given the same speech. Just talking about how important it is to people in their first jobs and recognizing that. I mean that's HUGE! You feel so small as an intern, or in your first job and you NEVER made me feel that way. You always made me feel like I could have a significant effect on the company from DAY ONE. And I did, by the was. But that is because of YOU. There is NO WAY I would've gotten to where I was, and have the skills that I have now if it weren't for you. I can't tell you how often I say to whomever is listening how blessed I was to have such amazing managers. You nurtured me—sometimes the lessons took longer than they would've for you, but I did learn them! Oh yes, I know you never liked to say that you were teaching anything...

There were two things I never said:

1. "So-and-so works *for* me."
2. "I will (or let me) teach you about this."

I find that both of these statements are pedantic and self-serving. I would say that "I work with so-and-so at MELA," and "Silly me, let me explain what I am talking about." Give people their pride and challenge them to grow into their positions, that is, to truly become a peer to a senior person. Also, young people don't want to be in need of being taught—it is just part of the condition; if they could do something about it, they would! I learned to do this by application of the Golden Rule—I never wanted to be considered subservient to anyone, and I was embarrassed if I needed to be taught, so I would not want it boldly announced. I also saw the effect it had on people—announcing them publicly in a way that connotes a peer relationship, with the CEO, made them so proud. Similarly, disguising the fact that they were junior and in need of learning the ropes inspired them to learn more quickly and ask questions.

Especially in a Growing Company

When a company is small, it is easy to have some sort of relationship with all of the employees. As the company grows, however, a special effort on the part of the leader is required. To do this correctly requires time and presence, things that are in short supply for the leaders of little companies with big ideas! Then why do it? You do it because it is good for business in the long run, best for the employees, and an excellent way to ensure that your values as leader are communicated.

Alexei

We hired this young engineer straight out of college. I took notice of him because he was very diligent and focused, and had great poise. He was also a daredevil who spent his weekends engaging in extreme sports like parachuting and mountain climbing. Initially, my interest in him was medical after he hurt his ankle doing something ill-advised. As I got to know him, it was readily apparent that he possessed excellent people skills; he was able to talk to anyone about anything, and he expressed himself quite well.

I approached the head of engineering and told him that I thought Alexei was a real winner and I wanted to help cultivate him and round out his knowledge of the company and the industry. His manager agreed and even realized that in time, it would be helpful for Alexei to follow the product out of development to commercialization. When I approached Alexei to ascertain his interest, he was concerned but anxious to see where this would lead. I told him that I read *Medical Device Daily* and wanted to send him some great articles for us to discuss once per week for an hour.

We began doing this every week, no matter how busy we were or what emergency cropped up. In fact, the crises were great for us to discuss relative to the *MDD* pieces. I explained many things about what I did, especially my interactions with doctors and investors, and how I would use a germane and current topic from *MDD* in my next meeting to emphasize something about what we were doing and why. He took everything in and started coming to our meetings with questions of his own. We built a great bond.

When I wrote to Alexei about this book and asked him to send me some of his insights, this is what he wrote:

I apologize for taking this long to reply—wanted to get my thoughts together. I think you picked a great subject to write a book about. From my experience, many managers I have come across have lacked proper skills and education to be effective leaders. Some leaders do have a natural gift of charisma and likable qualities, but everyone can use some proper education on the subject. Nothing is worse than a hard working professional who rises through the ranks to a managerial position and is completely unfit for the task. As I heard Vivian say once, "people don't leave jobs, they leave their bosses!" You certainly had the gift of leadership and it was evident from day one when I joined MELA. What makes humans different from other creatures of this planet is our desire to feel important. If you can make those around you feel important, they will blossom like spring flowers, and that is exactly what you were able to do.

Two examples, which stand out most in my memory, both happened during the first months of my employment. I remember when you invited me into your office and asked me if I would be interested in learning about the business strategies, the FDA, PMA, etc.—you made me feel very special (important). It was a beautiful gesture from my perspective, since it was my first job and I was somewhat scared, clueless of what to expect. It pushed me to read Medical Device Daily and to be more interested in the business aspects of the industry. I was proud to call home and tell my parents that the CEO of my company was having one-on-one weekly sessions with me, discussing business and the future of our company.

Second example, is when you decided to make me and Maceij softball team captains. It sounds silly, but it was a simple and effective way to show that we are useful/needed/important/liked. Having a CEO surrender his leadership (although it was just a softball

*game) and give it to two foreign kids who never played real softball,
showed us that you trust us (once again make us feel important).*

*There were other examples of course, when you gave me an
opportunity to experience the world of sales by asking me to help
with conferences, present to doctors, train medical staff, etc. They all
boil down to the same concept in my mind—you made me feel important, by treating me as someone above my actual experience level,
pushing me to be better and ultimately building my confidence. One
thing if I felt that you only treated me that way, but I have observed
you do exactly the same to majority of employees at MELA. Finally,
your care was evident through creating achievement recognition
awards and creative team building. Leaders with most loyal following are the ones that help everyone else around them succeed—they
"care" about those who work with them.*

Maybe Alexei should have written this book!

My favorite story involving Alexei happened on the day of our
FDA Advisory Committee Panel Meeting for MelaFind on November 18, 2010. This was the most trying experience of my life and
occurred in the middle of a year-long period during which I was really
suffering; I had lost nearly thirty pounds, was having five crying spells
per day, and was only able to sleep a couple of hours per night. (Read
*Innovation Breakdown—How the FDA & Wall Street Cripple Medical
Advances* for all of the details.) In an unbelievable turn of events that
represent the greatest fifteen minutes of my life (see Chapter 2), the
FDA Panel gave MelaFind their support, against all odds and in spite
of the FDA's unprecedented attacks and attempts to terminate the
product, and thereby, ruin the company. I was being inundated by
media, banking analysts, clinical experts, board members, lawyers,
and employees who were on-site at the public meeting. I had no
energy and was supporting myself by leaning against a wall, numb
and foggy. Alexei texted me from the company's offices, where the
employees were watching the AdComm meeting, and kept texting
me, despite my brief replies and commitment to discuss everything
with the company when I returned home. He wouldn't stop and his

words were emotionally charged. So I excused myself to go to the bathroom and found another wall to lean against to engage him.

ALEXEI: Joe, this was amazing; I have never seen anything like it.

JOE: Yes, amazing is the right word—when we get home, I want to hear what everyone was thinking and saying. See you on Monday.

ALEXEI: Joe, you don't understand, this CHANGED me!

JOE: Wow—I know, all of us down here are numb and depleted, we'll celebrate together on Monday.

ALEXEI: Joe, this was like watching *Gladiator*!

ALEXEI: I am serious.

ALEXEI: This should be a movie!

ALEXEI: That's it, I am calling Russell Crowe's agent now!

JOE: True, Maximus and I went into the Colosseum, against all odds, handicapped and beaten to face an evil Emperor! But, HE died! Don't call Crowe, call Clive Owen, he doesn't die in his movies!

ALEXEI: LOL! Yes, I will call Clive Owen's agent!

JOE: See you on Monday.

Alexei changed me. I will never forget those words and what they meant to me at the time, and still do today. Alexei went on to follow the product out of development into marketing and sales and was truly an all-star. He had intimate product knowledge and a love of the company. Why? Because we cared about him. (More on that softball game will be in Chapter 5.)

Transitions

I have run departments in large organizations as well as several small companies. Very small companies, like Antigen Express, which consisted of five people in a laboratory and me as the business and financing guy, are quite easy from a management perspective. Everyone is shoulder to shoulder, the goals are clear, and the sense of team is palpable. Anthra Pharmaceuticals was similar in the beginning; this time, there was no lab, just Denise Webber (head of clinical and data), a secretary, a couple of CRA's (clinical research associates), Al Thunberg, the CEO (who was remote), and me (President and COO). I noticed at Anthra that I could manage the company quite easily myself until we had thirteen employees. I was traveling quite a bit (about sixty percent of the time) in those days, but when we had twelve or less staffers, I had a strong connection to every employee, though not all of them reported to me directly. It seemed that even when there were problems or strife, the employees would wait until I got back into the office and allow me to broker some resolution. But, when we hired the thirteenth employee, poof, the company took an identity that I could not control by mere will. It became clear that management took a lot of work, and I needed HR help.

MELA Sciences was larger (twenty-two people) when I arrived, and I did not define the culture; the unique and gifted founders and original employees did. As time progressed and we hired more people, and some founders and old timers left, my influence increased to the point that we needed to take management very seriously, and we hired an excellent HR director named Vivian Yost, who taught our managers how to manage. She was my right hand so to speak—no one in the company, including me, was a pure manager, rather all of us had our own work to do so management tasks were relegated in importance. It was Vivian's job to not allow managers, including me, to abdicate their management responsibilities.

As we hired more and more capable senior employees, with Vivian on board, I noticed that the organization moved forward without my pushing it. However, I still insisted on meeting every prospective employee to whom we intended to make an offer of employment. I did this for many reasons, one of which may have been a control issue, for sure. But, I believe the real reason was that

I felt strongly that an offer of employment is a promise—the company is promising the employee that if he or she does what the job description says, the individual will be provided a rich and rewarding opportunity. I look at interviewing employees as a seduction—I want to make prospective employees love the company and if I want that strong of a commitment from them, they have the need and the right to interrogate the leader about the direction, culture, and priorities.

As Leela reflected on her interview at MELA and meeting with me:

> *I hope you're well and I hope I can help! I'm so glad you're writing this book. I apply your lessons daily, both consciously and subconsciously at this point! It's amazing to think of the lil' scared/naive/self-conscious girl I was when I walked into One Bridge Street and I met with you—your "office" in the back of the room and you had the guts of MelaFind on your desk. You showed me the LEDs, you gave me the run-down, and spoke about MelaFind like someone would speak about the excitement and anticipation of a first date.*

The rest is history...

I also will not offer a job to someone unless I feel that the company and I can deliver on what the person wants. The way I make that determination is by asking this question: "Other than a paycheck, what are you looking to get from this job?" I then reveal to the person why I am asking the question. I explain that if I do not feel we can deliver it to them within a year to eighteen months, it will not be a good fit because if they are good, they will be able to get a paycheck anywhere, but what will make them want to work and stay committed is if we can deliver to them whatever they really want. I then tell them that I am a talker, I do not believe in withholding information from employees in the name of confidentiality and because of that, at the very least, they will learn how a small company works and how their contribution fits into the whole mosaic we are building.

That exchange typically seals the deal and sets the ground rules and opportunity as I see it. I like having that talk with employees; for me, it establishes the unwritten employment agreement.

I went into the office one day after a week-long trip to Europe and I was greeted by Vivian and our head of marketing who were donning huge smiles. They told me that they had hired a new employee, a very recent magna cum laude graduate from Rutgers. They said they were afraid of losing her to another company if they didn't make her the offer, and so they did. This was the first (of many) employees to be hired without my involvement, and I was not thrilled because I hadn't met with her.

I went to say hello—she was very, very nervous and shy. By far, Jenna was the greenest employee that I ever employed. She had a sheltered upbringing in Northern Bergen County, N.J., similar to the kind that I had. She was a sponge; she was eager to learn without making it obvious that she needed to be taught. Oh, she would ask questions, but she had pride. And, she was very proper and reserved. Within her first few days, I asked for the *curriculum vitae* of a prospective candidate for another position at the company, and she looked at me quizzically, so I said, "It's a fancy way of saying resume." I went back to my office and then returned with a blank file on which I wrote Curriculum Vitae on the tab and I handed it to her. I told her to keep this in her drawer and every time she did something new, to put a record of it in the folder. I told her that in one year we would then review the items in the folder and draft a *curriculum vitae* for her. Throughout the year, I would often allude to the folder when I knew she did something for the first time and I would say, "Did you put a copy in the folder?"

My office was made of glass walls, and I had a six-foot glass table as my desk. I did this because I wanted people who visited my office to feel that we were working elbow to elbow, on the same team, and to feel like a peer. I hate the dynamic of someone sitting on the other side of the desk, many of which resemble thrones. It is intimidating for the person, and it screams of positional authority. I also don't like the ceremonial rising from the desk to join a visitor at a round table near the door. Who needs it? Space is at a premium—sitting at my desk with me saves time, money, and communicates so power-fully that we are united in our goals. I had several meetings per day, of course, with multiple parties. Whenever Jenna would come into my office she seemed so frightened, and she would always say that she did not mean to bother me. Bother me? This is my job!

Often, she would come with her colleagues in the marketing department, who were women. I would frequently preface some-thing important that I was about to say with, "Between us girls," as I leaned in and whispered. That would make all of them laugh, but none as much as Jenna, every time. One day, I realized that the dynamic was off—they were constantly looking to me for answers, yet I was relying on them for the answers. So I got up from my seat and I made whoever was leading the discussion of the topic at hand sit in my seat. I took a seat on the side of the table and put the head of marketing at the other head. One meeting was about travel and other logistics around our big trade show—this was Jenna's, and I made her sit in my chair, which she wound up doing a lot. I actu-ally instituted a new rule. At the start of any meeting with me, the youngest person in the room was required to take my seat; then, as the topics of the meeting shifted, the lead person took my chair.

I asked Jenna to provide some insights about her experiences regarding the value of selfless caring in business:

Hi Joseph! It's so nice to hear from you. Congratulations on starting to write another book. I think the theme of the book is perfect for you as I specifically remember you caring so much about the employees and managing us in the above mentioned ways. I've worked with a few CEO's now and you are by far the most unique, thoughtful, smart, and caring of them all. You always took the time to speak to us as a group and as individuals and would take the time to write intel-ligent, comprehensive, professional e-mails with complete thoughts and proper grammar! No other CEOs that I've worked with have done those things—I've worked with five.

A few of my experiences and lessons:

"Opportunity lies outside of your comfort zone"—I remember all the times you made me speak in front of the group at company meetings when the head of the Marketing department wasn't around (or even when my boss was there). I wasn't comfortable doing this as one of the youngest employees in the company, but I knew that it was a good public speaking lesson and taught me to be prepared at all times! I think speaking in front of the company also helped people respect me and take me seriously even though I was very young. It showed that YOU trusted and respected me enough to share my thoughts in front of the company. At that time, speaking in front of the group felt like torture, but looking back I'm really glad you gave me the opportunity and I understand the reason.

"You want to be someone that someone would want to go to lunch with"—you said it more eloquently. I don't think those were the exact words, but it stuck with me! Every work experience or even personal experience I face that is unique and enriching I consciously try to keep in my memory bank to use for storytelling. I would always love hearing your stories and I know they come with age and experience. You always had interesting and funny things to say and shared so much to try to teach those around you, especially me. This is still one of my goals: to be someone interesting enough to take to lunch (not dinner, anyone can be interesting over dinner and drinks lol). You took me to lunch at Red Hat when you told me this, and I remember the other marketing ladies being so jealous that you took me and didn't ask them! This made me feel special and important. Actually your professional storytelling lesson taught me that storytelling is a critical asset in business. Everyone loves a good story and I noticed that all the execs that I've worked with spend a ton of time telling their own stories.

During my first week of work, you asked me to schedule a Research and Development meeting, but you just said "R&D" (this is when I was assistant/marketing coordinator). Being very GREEN and fresh out of college, I didn't even know what R&D meant. I knew I was working at a medical device start-up company, but all of the terminology was new to me. I sent a meeting request for an "Rnd" meeting having no idea it meant "Research & Development" and it should have been written as "R&D." As soon as I sent the meeting request, you immediately called me into your office and I was so scared because I knew I did something wrong and I didn't know what I was doing. You asked me if I knew what it meant, and I said "NO" (I was so embarrassed). You didn't laugh or make me feel bad about it, but you took this as an opportunity to teach me my first Joseph lesson. You acted as a teacher writing things on the white board and explaining the difference between "R&D" and "Commercialization." You were the CEO and had so much on your plate at that time (we just submitted the PMA application), but somehow you took the time to explain to me the meaning of R&D for almost an hour. I will never forget that time.

One day I had a meeting in the city with our PR company, and was super busy working on marketing/PR activities with Claudia. I don't know why you did this, but you asked me to write an e-mail to the BOD explaining all the marketing activities we were working on and our preparation plans for the American Academy of Dermatology (AAD) trade show. I was surprised you didn't ask Claudia to do this, but she wasn't the type of manager that would be mad that you asked me instead of her. I was so nervous to write an e-mail to the BOD, and again, uncomfortable. I dropped everything else I was doing to write this e-mail. I remember working on it for a couple hours to make it perfect, even though I had a million other things to do. Anything having to do with the BOD always made me nervous, of course, but I wrote a very long e-mail and you sent it directly to the BOD without blinking an eye. I remember getting a lot of compliments on the e-mail from the BOD. That made me feel really confident and important and at that moment I realized why you asked me to do it. You wanted it to be another learning experience for me and you wanted to give me another opportunity for the higher-ups to respect me and show my value as an employee.

"Never ask for permission, ask for forgiveness." I use this line all the time and I believe it to be true because I have seen it work inside and outside of work. I can't think of specific example of this, but I often use this motto.

"The fish stinks from the head." You would say this when you felt bad decisions were made in the company or when an employee messed up. You would blame yourself as our leader. At another company where I worked, I had an awful boss who was extremely negative with a gloomy outlook on everything (professionally and personally). I think this directly impacted the marketing initiatives we worked on and my overall attitude about my job and the company. Ultimately I decided to leave because that wasn't the type of environment in which I wanted to spend my days.

"It's good to be King!"—Ha-ha I love this one! Being in charge you get to make all the decisions and reap the benefits of success the most!

MELA Awards—Somehow I think I won more awards than anyone else in the company and I can't help but think that you had something to do with that! Even though we were so small, you made people feel important in a big way.

Taking me to the FDA panel meeting and the NASDAQ opening bell events were also memories with you that I will never forget and I am so grateful that I was able to be a part of them.

Never end a sentence with a preposition—it actually isn't wrong to do, but you hated when people would do this. For some reason I remembered and always make an effort to avoid doing this, still! Not a big deal, it's just grammar, but a vivid memory of mine.

Great wines I learned from you... Ferrari Carano Chardonnay, Conundrum Chardonnay, Navarro Correas Malbec

These are the good ole' days—you don't know you are in the good old days until they are over! This is so true. I Googled this line and it's actually from the finale of the show "The Office," but I'll still give you credit for it anyway!

These are just a few things, but I really loved how much you cared and made me feel very important as one of your youngest, greenest employees. I would always share my MELA stories with my parents and friends and they always told me how lucky I was to work at MELA and for someone like you. My MELA days with you as the CEO were the most enriching and exciting and my job felt so real and impactful.

Jenna discussed some items that I had forgotten. The reason that I took Jenna to lunch was because I did not interview her before she was hired, so I wanted to get those points across to her in a non-threatening and supportive fashion now that she was an employee. My goal in life, which I communicated to Jenna, was to be so interesting as to be someone with whom others would want to have lunch.

While the team was at another AAD meeting a couple of years later, I told Jenna and Diana that I wanted them to sit with me at the dinner we were planning. We were transitioning from an R&D company to a commercialization company, and we were going to be meeting prospective customers for the first time. One of our Board members, Anne Egger, invited the guests, and we really did not know who was coming. I wanted to show Jenna and Diana how to engage experts with whom we had no experience. Well, Jenna and Diana sent me an email when the dinner started stating that they were exhausted from setting-up the exhibit and all of the preparation up to that point, so they asked whether they could skip the dinner. I said that would be okay. They copied the head of marketing on the email, who was shocked, apparently, as I was told later. He approached Jenna and explained that when the CEO wants you to sit next to him so that he can show you something, you don't say no. He told Jenna that the company, while small now, would soon be much larger and opportunities to have that kind of time with the CEO will be gone. Jenna said to him that Joseph will always make time to have lunch with us! She was right.

MELA Awards were something that Vivian and I implemented. At the monthly company meetings, we would hand out an award—certificate and $50 gift card—to one or two employees determined by the management committee to have particularly exhibited a valued behavior over the past month. The way it worked was that any employee or manager could nominate someone—there was a form that required specific reasons and supporting rationale. Then, the management committee (all department heads and me) would vote. The award categories changed as the needs of the company and culture dictated. Five of my favorite behaviors were: (1) helps others succeed, (2) takes initiative as if he/she owned the company, (3) acknowledges unsatisfactory outcomes and rapidly corrects, (4) integrates departments outside of his/her area, and (5) fills voids no matter where they exist. These five behaviors more than any of the others embodied the culture that I wanted at the company. Yes, Jenna won many MELA Awards, mostly for two reasons—she was constantly being nominated for awards by members of out-side departments because she was excellent and she cared; and she adapted her behaviors to fit the needs of the company. Jenna became the ideal employee—she took pride in her work, did a great job, anticipated needs, and saw past the pettiness. And, these behaviors were from someone who was the youngest employee! The only time that Jenna would ever vocalize something that disturbed her was when she was pressed to do so at the year-end review...talk about low maintenance.

Jenna also mentioned the Panel meeting, which I discussed in detail in Chapter 2. We had about ten employees at the meeting while the rest of the company was back at the office. The marketing team—Diana, Jenna, and the head of the department—attended and sat in the audience; they were not part of the on-site two days and nights of preparation or the presentations, however they did develop the physician training module, which I would be presenting at the Panel meeting. It was important for them to see how the panel reacted to our data because they devised the final positioning and messaging.

At the lunchtime intermission, things were dire. As we came up to start the afternoon session, Jenna and Diana were standing at the top of the stairs just in front of the entrance to the meeting room. Jenna saw me, looked like she was about to cry, and took a few rapid steps toward me. I could not engage with her because I was completely depleted and I needed to speak with our experts before the call to order, so I put my hand up like a traffic cop giving a stop sign. I know that I looked incredibly serious and determined—I did not even make eye contact or smile, which is very rare for me. The afternoon session was an outright disaster—even worse than the situation at lunch. I thought to myself how this must be killing all of our staff, so I craned my neck panning the audience looking for Jenna and Diana to see how they were doing. And, when we made eye contact, I smiled at them—why, I don't know; there was absolutely nothing to smile about. I wanted them to know that they were on my mind and that we were all in this together.

When we got back to the office after the ridiculously dramatic turn of events culminating in a positive vote, we had a company meeting. Everyone wanted to hear from me, about the fifteen-minute final summation. I wanted this to be a team-building exercise, so I said that I was going to be selfish here: I wanted to hear what I missed, that is, I wanted people to share their individual experiences and do so with the entire company so that everyone can own it. I wanted to hear what was going on in the planning and execution group in the war room during the afternoon (Kathy and Leela), what was going on from the perspective of the audience (Jenna and Diana), what was going on with the investors (Richard), and what was happening at the office (Nyq, Alexei and others). It was an amazing company meeting, one that I will never forget. Jenna told three stories, the longest of which was about my putting my hand up when she and Diana simply wanted to tell me that they believed in me and what we were doing no matter what the FDA was saying, and then looking back at Diana and her later—she made the point of how touched she was that I put her first in the middle of all that was going-on. She wrote-out her narrative because she did not want to forget to mention anything.

Jenna's earlier comments to me also mentioned one of my favorite phrases—ask for forgiveness, not permission. I am glad that she remembered that one and uses it. This is very important for people who have great insights and a command of their facts, but are somehow intimidated to such an extent that they do not believe their opinions are valid. I impressed this lesson on another employee in whom I invested a great amount of time and whom I greatly admire, Leela (see Chapter 6). She expressed a similar sentiment to me when I asked her for comments:

> *Ask for forgiveness not permission—I'm sure I'm bastardizing so many of these lessons! This really goes into just being PROACTIVE, seeing the bigger picture and doing whatever you can to make it happen. Again, I hate to keep bringing it back to post-Gulfo world but I truly take these lessons with me. I've been so frustrated with my friend for not listening to MY lessons in terms of how to make things happen in her job. Like, instead of waiting for an executive to tell you that the band isn't adding anything (just an example), ask the question FIRST and say this is what we're going to do to add to the show. I guess it goes along with risk-taking, but I think it's essential in being*

successful. You taught me that and I feel you also gave me the confi-
dence to know when to follow my gut and not ask you permission for
everything. Thinking about it now, asking permission for everything
is a really easy way NOT to take responsibility for anything.

There is one thing that I am grateful that Jenna did not remember—the time that I told her she did a "piss poor" job and that I was
disappointed in her. It turned out that I was operating on erroneous facts and I made a hasty and emotional conclusion. I was dead
wrong, and I apologized to her immediately, and repeatedly. Just
because I selflessly cared doesn't mean that I was perfect. But,
thankfully, selflessly caring does create a deep reservoir of good will
with employees.

Reaching Out for Help

Many executives who have reached the top of the pyramid use that
as the validation for all of their behaviors. We are all victims of our
most recent experiences, and successful people are victims of their
successes. The day that a manger believes that his way is the best
way or that there is nothing wrong with her approach or style is the
day that the person needs to resign and just pet the dog all day. I have
been on the other end of this thinking, having a CEO who believes
the culture or mood or *modus operandi* of the company is the fault
of the employees. I remember a management exercise early in my
career where the CEO basically said this at the kick-off: the management consultants were there to fix and align us because we were
flawed, you see. Utter nonsense.

All of us are in a state of becoming. I selflessly cared to be the
best leader I could be—every interaction with employees and every
project makes me better if I seek to learn from it and if I audit my
performance and obtain feedback.

While I was CEO of MELA Sciences, my workload and management responsibilities became too difficult for me to manage. Vivian,

the HR head, explained that I was inserting myself into too many things and spreading myself too thin. I didn't want to hear it, but she kept bringing it to my attention by pointing to instances that demonstrated my approach was neither efficient or effective. Finally, I exclaimed that I did not know any other way to do it, so she recommended that I get a coach and we brought in Julie Kantor. Vivian and Julie changed my approach and my life. They taught me how to delegate, and Vivian set up employee training sessions on a variety of management topics including management by objectives and conducting meetings. Vivian and Julie taught me how to be a more effective manager—they got me to let go of the emotion and disappointment I would feel when a good job was not delivered, to be explicit in my instructions to my direct reports, and they also taught me the appropriate way to provide feedback that is actionable.

My wife, Adele, has been a senior executive at several large Fortune 100 companies. She undergoes management training and team building exercises regularly; she frequently shares with me what happens during these sessions. Having worked in small companies, I haven't had the luxury of such training. I understand that if I am an apple and Bridgette is a pear, I have to think like a pear, not an apple, to resonate with Bridgette, but I have never undergone the training, so I don't know what to do with oranges!

I wanted to provide an impactful training program to all of our employees, so I asked Adele which of all the exercises in which she has been involved would be the best. She recommended the coach Martha Borst, whom we brought in for a day-and-a-half session. I participated with the managers, rather than taking the position that I am not in need of learning team-building tips. I had to do and say some uncomfortable things in front of employees about things that frighten me and my weaknesses. I did it. I realized that I was making myself vulnerable, that the information that I conveyed could be used by employees against me or to manipulate me, but I did not let that stop me. I selflessly cared enough to let myself be exposed, to be raw and vulnerable. I gained something out of it, and so did the employees, some of whom continue to stay in touch with Martha.

Learning with Your Employees

My first significant management position was in 1992 at Cytogen Corporation, a cutting-edge biotech company. A twenty-year-old friend of Sue Mesday, who worked in the department, interviewed to work with me as an administrative assistant. Jean Slayback-Mantuano was nervous, but tough and stoic. We offered her the job and she worked with me for four years—we literally grew up together in the business. Jean was very strong-willed and proud. I haven't seen Jean for twenty years but she sent me the following note when I asked for her thoughts on caring in business:

I don't know if you realize how positively you affected my career simply through small gestures, respect for others, genuinely caring about people and through an approachable demeanor—things that seemed to all come naturally for you.

I thank you for taking a chance with me by giving me the opportunity to join the Clinical team at Cytogen. I was young and moderately experienced, but I had no knowledge of clinical studies, R&D, or biotech, and certainly no understanding of monoclonal antibodies! You made it a point to change all of that. You took the time to explain things to me beginning at a very basic level and taught me about the development of drugs from investigational stage through FDA approval. You also gave me opportunities to be creative and trusted my judgment. From there, my career was launched in the biotech/pharma arena and for that I'm forever grateful.

Not only were you instrumental in launching my career, but you also supported the pursuit of my undergrad degree at night. Actually, simply put, you more than supported me with one class in particular. I was pretty much failing philosophy, and you spent quite a bit of time to help me with that class and to earn a passing grade. I know that you were passionate about this subject from your past studies, and I always admired your devout faith. You enjoyed teaching and sharing your knowledge no matter what the subject matter was.

To this day, I always remember that you never said that I worked "for" you. Rather you always said we worked together or you worked with me. This is something that I carried with me through my career, and as I moved along and had the opportunity to manage people, I never said someone worked for me but with me. It makes a difference—it is another example of your respect for others and really means a lot.

Some of the fun stuff that still makes me chuckle:

- ▶ *I consider you highly intelligent. However, to this day, I can't believe you didn't know that cats licked themselves as part of their regular grooming, and wow, did that ever repulse you. I don't think you're fond of cats.*

- ▶ *Talking to Adele about shoes.*

- ▶ *When I went to Los Angeles for spring break one year, you told me to call you if I needed someone to bail me out of jail. You were serious...*

- ▶ *When you gave me a hard time, I'd threaten to change your hotel reservations to a much less-than-desirable lodging option.*

Jean went on to several large biopharma companies and had a great career in communications. We invested time in each other, and we both seemed to have benefited. We remembered what we learned while working together, and how we applied these lessons in the future. Most of our careers were spent apart, but we are forever joined from the common experience so early in our careers.

CHAPTER 4

Make Difficult Decisions

Making decisions is the job of all managers. Many seek to make as few decisions as possible for fear of repercussions that could damage their careers or make them less popular with their direct reports. However, I believe that a manager gains tremendous credibility with his peers and with the troops when he is unafraid to take the lead in making difficult decisions. The manager will further his cause when he takes the time to explain why.

Especially when the leader is new to the team (new department head or CEO), it is in making difficult decisions and in his conduct dealing with the aftermath, repercussions, and next steps that he becomes part of the team, earns respect, engenders personal leadership, and gains followers. To put it another way, the leader needs to earn his position on the team and there is no better way to do that than to perform.

Staying the Course

A little over a year after joining MELA Sciences, a huge setback occurred with our breakthrough medical system. I had been busy working with the Food & Drug Administration on securing a clear path forward with respect to the appropriate clinical study needed to provide definitive proof and to serve as the basis of approval of our lead product, MelaFind, an early melanoma detection device. We were successful and subsequently launched the pivotal trial in patients with atypical pigmented skin lesions. Unfortunately, shortly after starting the study, we had to stop it because the prototype devices being used in the study were not robust enough. This issue was an engineering challenge, as opposed to medical or regulatory challenges; I am not an engineering expert.

I was faced with a critical decision—leave the company or stay to fix the problem. For me, the best option would be to leave because I had achieved an excellent and rare milestone (a binding protocol agreement with the FDA), and I could avoid the drama and uncertainty of trying to manage a re-engineering effort. I knew, however, that if I had left, the company would have closed down, either immediately or within six months. I was only with the company for about a year, so I had not developed deep roots. In fact, I was an outsider to the core group, which had been together in this company, as well as in prior lives, for many years before I arrived. I was an interloper, someone forced upon them by investors. As CEO, of course, I felt some responsibility; however, I was told that the engineering was complete when I accepted the position, and the engineering aspects were being managed by expert engineers in the core founding group, not by me, as agreed from the start of my tenure. I was focusing on the clinical and regulatory issues, and I delivered in a big way. The easy and correct decision for me was to leave and to never look back.

I didn't go.

This one decision put into motion a series of events that forever changed me. For the good of many others, including patients, early investors, employees, founders, and other stakeholders, I knowingly entrenched myself into a morass of uncertainty and complexity that would make me do what I vowed to stop doing just one year earlier—fighting! Having had some successes in my career prior to coming to MELA, I decided that I no longer needed to fight, no longer had to play Sisyphus in rolling a boulder up a hill whose summit would never be reached. I had paid my dues and I now wanted to "cash-in," so to speak. Well, the next eight and one half years turned out to be a fifteen round heavyweight brawl that almost killed me.

This one difficult decision brought more difficult moves:

1. Selecting the appropriate core team members to solve the problems while letting others go;
2. Deciding to partner with an expert optics designer in Germany rather than continue to do it in-house in New York;
3. Against the will of the entire company, deciding to divest a dental product (DIFOTI, that detected cavities with light) in order to conserve resources and focus on the lead product, MelaFind;
4. Deciding to take the company public to raise the funds necessary to redesign the product;
5. Ordaining a young, unproven brilliant algorithm developer as project team leader;
6. Moving the company into different space against the will of some of the most critical leaders of the effort—the "secret sauce" and "key ingredient;"
7. Reorganizing the company, changing reporting structures, as well as hiring and firing;
8. Filing supervisory review requests against the FDA;
9. Filing a citizen petition against the FDA; and
10. Engaging in a public relations and medical battle with the FDA to obtain approval of MelaFind.

It was in the middle of these very trying times that I earned the respect of the founding team—I showed them that I was not afraid to make difficult decisions and that I was in the thick of it with them.

I also showed them that in addition to being "the manager," I delivered in ways that others on the team could not.

Employees and managers notice, especially if the leader is transparent. I firmly believe that there is very, very little that is truly confidential in a company. Many managers use knowledge as power. I don't. I feel that if you over-communicate with employees, you receive incredible dividends. Think about it—you want your employees to eat, drink, sleep, and breathe their work. You want them to be anxious to show up in the morning—I call that "speeding to work." You want them to "think out of the box." One of the best ways to achieve this is by sharing information with them and inviting them to think about the whole project and company.

And, so I did—employees saw virtually everything. I would explain to them the challenges and the horns of the dilemma; I would take their varied input; and I would justify the tack I took. I treated every employee as my peer. I would also let them know when I was wrong—in making this many tough decisions, you are not going to get all of them right!

In fact, you will get a lot wrong. I encouraged them to tell me when they thought I got things wrong. One of the things I truly enjoyed was when an employee would come to me without any reservations whatsoever, and tell me about something I said at a company meeting, or something I did that was not appropriate in their opinions. This gave me an opportunity to first learn, then to engage them and stoke their passion for the company and their job. And, sometimes, I needed to apologize.

In fact, we created a core value and behavior—admitting when something is not going well. I had to do my share of admitting, and fast correcting. This created a company culture in which mistakes were not only tolerated, but even encouraged to the extent that they are committed in an effort to tackle difficult challenges and they are quickly acknowledged and fixed. If you are not making tough decisions, not taking risks to optimize, you will not be making mistakes.

Employees also saw how much I cared by having front row seats to the difficult decisions and the battles. Because I was an over-communicator, they often had third-person omniscient insights into the facts of the matters I was confronting. This was very inspiring to them. The single most competent professional that I hired into MELA was Jeff Wallace, an expert in software and algorithm verification and validation, as well as hardware development and quality systems. He had been consulting for us for several years and twice per year I tried to hire him to lead all of R&D. Apparently, making tough decisions and fighting wore him down—he told me that after four years of seeing how much I cared and how much I had endured to get the company to where it was, he now wanted to join, which he did. If Jeff did not join full time, we would never had been able to launch the product. As he reflected:

I consulted for EOS/MELA for four years and during this duration I was approached by Joseph several times to join the company as a full-time employee, however I was reluctant and continued to turn him down. I'm the type of individual who has to assure that there will be some level of impact and the management that I would report to had the necessary passion and focus that could take it to that expert level. During the battle, and I mean battle, with the FDA I truly saw something amazing in Joseph. He had the passion, strength, and drive to push through a barricade guarded by 5 million men to overcome the necessary evils. This was a definite turning point for me, so the next time Joseph asked if I would come aboard, I said yes and indicated that I was doing this for him and of course the reasons why.

Difficult Decisions Beget Difficult Decisions

As mentioned above, at MELA we were faced with a major crisis within a year of my joining. The MelaFind system prototypes were not made of sufficient quality to be used in the pivotal trial for FDA approval. The founding team did a phenomenal job in the research,

82

prototyping, and early development, but they were not skilled at late-stage development. Since I am not an engineer, I could not step in and take over the effort. I needed to manage and lead the company through this crisis without specific and direct knowledge of the details. This is not what I signed up to do, of course, and the situation was very distressing. A board member identified a well-known electro-optical company in Ohio that could dive-in and identify the problems that had to be addressed. We engaged the firm, and a month later we realized what we were up against—some fixes were simple, but most were not. Rather this was going to take a lot more time and money than anyone, including the investors and myself, thought.

Ohio could help us solve the problems, but it did not want to manufacture the systems. We found a company in Michigan that was eager to manufacture MelaFind once all of the procedures for doing so were final and validated, but it did not want to engage in what is called "methods development." So one option was to have Ohio re-engineer the system and then develop the manufacturing methods that would be transferred to Michigan, which would produce the final systems.

There was another choice—a group in Germany named Askion that developed and manufactured precision electro-optical systems (see Chapter 1). It was run by Lutz Doms, an engineer who had worked at Bayer Diagnostics, and was spun off by Zeiss about ten years previously. Among other things, Askion manufactured and serviced Agfa's one-hour photo machines. Askion represented the best elements of both Ohio and Michigan for our purposes—a real R&D laboratory to engage in design-for-manufacturing experiments *and* optimization, and more formal, buttoned-up, large scale manufacturing.

Askion also had something that neither Ohio nor Michigan had—a significant appetite for the project. The company was hungry for business and told us it was prepared to be our partner in the *entire* process going forward. It would give us a complete characterization of the prototype systems that we developed and had used in clinical studies to date. The firm would undertake a major redesign for manufacturing of all elements of the camera. It would develop robust manufacturing methods and precision fixtures. And the firm would guarantee commercial grade manufacturing under both ISO (European) and FDA (USA) guidelines. Askion also agreed to house several of our employees within its facility, something that Ohio wouldn't do. The company estimated that we would need at least a year, if not two, to make the systems for use in our pivotal trial—systems that, if successful, could then be manufactured at scale with great quality.

By the end of March 2005 then, I had an excellent idea of the problems, comfort that the true breakthrough elements of the system were solid, and three alternatives for partners to get it all done—Ohio, Michigan, and Askion. What to do? Should I have the company work with one group on design for manufacturing development (Ohio), and another on manufacturing (Michigan)? Or should I have it work with a hungry group that would do both but was also an ocean apart with significant cultural and political differences from our founding team? And regardless of what I chose, would the founders act out against me or respond to my leadership on the issue? The pressure was on, and I needed to make a decision.

The board agreed with my recommendation to proceed with Askion; I then asked Tomek (our optical engineer who designed the lens composed of 10 elements) and Nyq to move to Germany during the design-for-manufacturing process. (Tomek remained in Germany until he left the company in 2013.) I personally spent a week per month at Askion for just less than two years. The challenge was not actually to build a *better* system, but rather a mass-producible handheld that matched the optical properties of the first three generations of prototypes, called T1, T2, and T3 handhelds used in clinical studies to date. This is an important point: when you're starting from scratch, better is, well... better. But because we weren't starting from scratch, we didn't actually want Askion to make our design better or use better materials, because those would have provided us with a completely different optical profile. And a totally different optical profile wouldn't match the optical profile upon which the algorithms were developed, and the vast clinical data we had amassed to date. We needed the new systems made with reliable, reproducible, and scalable methods, but with a final product that still matched the optical profile of the T1, T2, and T3 prototypes. We needed *new, reliable, and robust* but not *better*. Otherwise, we'd have to start from square one, which would have taken even more time and more money!

There was much Sturm und Drang in the process, and Nyq would often show me examples of how the new handheld prototypes were not consistent with T1-3, and then I would have to mediate those battles. That is, when I wasn't doing the rest of my job, which included attending banking conference presentations, managing the team back in New York, dealing with the board, maintaining goodwill with the dermatology community, and eventually overseeing the rebooted clinical studies to validate the new prototypes.

The effort was daunting and many impasses emerged. On several occasions when Nyq would come to me explaining how decisions that were being made on the hardware end were jeopardizing the consistency of the new system relative to the old, I asked him to become the Project Team Leader. He refused, repeatedly. I explained to him that the project would be completed more quickly and efficiently if he were to do it. I told him that since he was on the ground in Germany, shoulder to shoulder with the guys in the trenches, he was the natural fit. Nyq hates authority and the last thing that he wanted to do was become "the man," so to speak. Also, his expertise is software and algorithms, not hardware, even though he builds robots in his spare time. We spoke every day and he would often get quite animated with respect to the recalcitrance of the consultant who was leading the effort with the Askion team. I told Nyq that when he was ready to become Project Team Leader, I would dismiss the consultant.

Life is the interplay of forces; when the force of Nyq's anger over the ill-informed decisions that were being made exceeded the force of Nyq's resistance to take over as Project Team Leader, I got what I wanted. Nyq called me and told me he was ready to lead the entire effort at Askion. I promptly called our consultant and informed him of my decision and thanked him for his help.

Nyq made a very difficult decision, one with which he was never quite comfortable. I supported and coached him, but he had his own style which he never altered. I was betting on his success so I supported him completely. This annoyed some employees, particularly one highly accomplished hire we made a year or so later. However, I stuck with Nyq at every turn. And, it paid off.

The team at Askion, led by Nyq, made major contributions to the product, including changing the optical path from ninety degrees to a linear 180 degrees, designing a new optical block that matched the properties of the folded block, partnering with Zeiss to make the lens, and creating precision fixtures for highly controlled and reproducible manufacturing. Tomek worked hand-in-hand with the Askion hardware team, and Nyq developed all of the manufacturing software that controlled assembly, testing, and release, in addition to the algorithms that made the system operate. The fact that Askion was inspected by the FDA, approved as a manufacturing facility by both the FDA and European Union, and that MelaFind was subsequently approved for use in patients a few years later speaks volumes about the many, many difficult decisions that we made.

Funding is Never an Easy Decision, or an Easy Process

In development-stage companies, the single biggest problem is money. With no product on the market generating sales, how do you fund huge research and development projects that may not pan out? You sell stock, that is, issue equity in the company. What happens

when there are setbacks and when the plan that the private investors were literally betting on is no longer viable? That is exactly what
happened with the re-engineering effort, described above. Getting
MelaFind to the point of FDA approval was going to take much more
time and money than anyone anticipated.

I'd already been talking to a number of venture capitalists in
February and March 2005 about investing in MELA. We had the
perfect profile for a blue chip venture capitalist to consider as an
investment. First, we had enrolled several thousand patients in
Phase 2 clinical studies that showed the product worked. Second,
the regulatory risk had been taken off the table by virtue of the binding protocol agreement with the FDA. Third, we had the support of
top melanoma experts in the form of key opinion-leader dermatologists. Fourth, the fundamental technology had just been vetted by a
significant technical review by leading electro-optical contractors.
Fifth, I had an engineering partner in mind to finalize the product
and make final systems for the pivotal trial and then commercial
production. And sixth, there was the high unmet medical-need dis-
ease-state. Our product addressed a real life-or-death need. What
else did they need to know?

Several venture capitalists were interested, and I was pushing them to step up with a meaningful investment. And then I got
a phone call from Jonathan Burklund, a banker I had known back
in my days at Anthra, with whom I'd lost contact. He'd tracked me
down by searching for me on the Internet, and he'd also done some
research on MELA and was extremely impressed. I took him through
the same pitch I was giving the venture capitalists, and told him that
I was convinced that with the mistakes behind us, the only thing left
was execution risk. His response? "Let me take you public." WHAT?

Burklund proceeded to tell me that he'd just raised $35 million
in the public markets for a company called CABG Medical, which was
developing an artificial graft for bypass surgery. Manny Villafana, a
well-known serial entrepreneur, headed the company, so it had that

going for it, but it also only had data from trials in *pigs*—not humans. Burklund said that CABG could have raised $50 million if it wanted to, and he felt that he'd just palpated a soft spot in the public markets for medtech companies that promised returns similar to venture capital investing. He said that MELA represented far less risk but an equal return to an investor who might be looking at a biotech IPO. (Or a CABG Medical IPO, for that matter: CABG was dissolved in 2006 when the technology failed in FDA trials.)

I told him that I would think about it. But that didn't take long, because the venture capitalist with whom I had been closest to moving forward soon told me that all investments were on hold pending administrative changes at the highest levels of his fund. I called Burklund and told him that I wanted to present the idea of going public to the board of MELA. He came to the next board meeting in June 2004 and we did just that.

The three directors representing the $9 million that had just been invested in the company on my joining discussed it with their angel network. They liked the idea in principle, but they and the rest of the board didn't think that I'd be able to get it done. Without a viable alternative, though, they agreed to let me go ahead and try.

Dina and I went on the IPO roadshow in late July and early August of 2005 while our chief financial officer managed the SEC review of the S-1 with the lawyers. The seven main points we made on our roadshow were:

1. Our founders, off-the-charts geniuses who had developed computer vision systems used by the Pentagon, had created a device for melanoma detection that worked, based on clinical data from 2,000 patients to date. That addressed the notion of *technology risk*;

2. We had a very rare and legally binding protocol agreement that covered all of the critical items for subsequent approval determination, most notably the parameters for proving

safety and effectiveness. The agreement protected us from staff changes, leadership changes, and political changes at the FDA, and in doing so addressed *regulatory risk*;

3. I, Joe Gulfo, had been responsible for the approval and launch of a number of products and I had managed two advisory panels, so I showed a solid profile when it came to *execution risk*;

4. A group in Germany, the optics capital of the world, was going to manufacture MelaFind, which addressed *production risk*;

5. Some of the best and most renowned melanoma experts in the world were participating in the program, which addressed *medical risk*;

6. Dermatology was (and remains) a booming specialty and there was a completely unfulfilled and significant medical need. That took care of *business risk*, and so;

7. There was only one risk left, Mr. Investor. That was *financing risk*, and that is what we're asking you to help us address.

We visited close to fifty funds all over the country with our bankers. We thought it was a great pitch, and many institutional investors seemed to agree.

Everything seemed to be going well. And then we started hearing rumors that Ladenburg Thalmann, our lead manager (banker), might be getting out of the investment banking business or be acquired. Ladenburg had just done a great deal for CABG Medical, and its chairman was a well-known and successful pharmaceutical executive, Dr. Phil Frost, so the news was certainly a surprise. But nothing had been easy so far, so why should we have thought the IPO process would be any different?

When we finished the IPO roadshow, the funds that were interested made it clear that they wouldn't participate in a deal in which the lead manager's future was unknown. So we had to suspend the process, wait until after Labor Day, choose a new lead manager, give the firm time to perform its diligence, update the S-1, and then go out again. In late September and early October, ThinkEquity, our new lead manager, accompanied us to another fifty or so presentations, a little more than half of which we made to the very same investors we'd visited on the first go-around.

In retrospect, this turn of events probably sounds straightforward enough and is surely something that other companies have had to deal with in the past. That much is true—we weren't the first, and we won't be the last. But it wasn't as simple as finding a new co-pilot because the first one had fallen sick. We had on our hands what bankers call a "broken deal." And broken deals leave a horrible taint. Even though it wasn't me (or anyone else at MELA) that broke it, we ended up the ones who smelled. It doesn't really matter how you got there; if your deal is broken, your company is suddenly "flawed" in a real and meaningful way. At the conclusion of the first roadshow, we were eyeing a ten dollar per share price, which would have meant a $50 million IPO. With the taint of a broken deal, investor demand fell to such an extent that at the end of the second roadshow, we were looking at just six or seven dollars per share. And nothing whatsoever had changed inside the company.

We'd planned on pricing after the close of trading on Tuesday, September 27. After making calls to all of the funds that had expressed interest, ThinkEquity's capital markets honcho informed me that he couldn't put a deal together and apologized for having wasted our time. What the hell? We'd given the funds exactly what they'd asked for—new bankers and a significantly reduced offering price. And now the deal was dead? I was crushed, angry, and shocked all at once. The company would be shut down, no doubt.

I took the red eye from San Francisco to New York and couldn't sleep a wink. At 8:30 a.m., I was working out on a Stairmaster, my heart rate in the 160s, when my phone rang. It was one of the private investors who'd played a part in hiring me. He asked me what I was doing. I replied, "Trying to kill myself in a socially acceptable manner!" Once I'd blown off some steam, I called the bankers in San Francisco and told them, with great passion, that what MELA was doing was important and we simply could not fail. I told them that we had to take another run at it, and I needed the list of all of the funds that were warm to us so that I could win over them. The bankers thought I was nuts, but gave me the list anyway. And I started dialing (and visiting) for dollars.

One of the funds was full of very smart and shrewd guys who had played good cop/bad cop and bad cop/worse cop with us during pricing discussions. I implored them, sharing my passion and vision as best I could. I kept hounding them over the next few days and managed to get them speaking to the bankers again. At that point, though, they insisted that the deal be limited to a certain number of investors with every single one committing some minimum amount. They also wanted some insider participation. In other words, they wanted a very "tight" deal. In IPO financings, they told me, the concern was that some funds would come in simply to get the stock on the cheap. Assuming it traded up—which bankers practically promise you will happen while they're trying to convince you to take an even steeper discount than they'd originally said was necessary—one or more of them would then vacate their position, having made their fast money "playing the deal," and leaving others holding the bag.

It's hard to overemphasize the preposterousness of hearing this from them. These were the same people who had driven the price down from twelve dollars at the start of the first roadshow to ten dollars at the end of that process, and also the ones who then drove it down to six or seven dollars during the second roadshow. And now they were worried about other less "principled" investors simply looking to flip our stock? But that's where we found ourselves, and we had to do what we had to do. They eventually came in for $5 million worth of stock, at $5 per share. And a few others followed. We got the deal done on October 12. Despite the lower-than-hoped-for stock price, it was a victory. There was only one other publicly traded, pre-revenue medical device company at the time, NxStage Medical.

MELA started trading at five dollars per share on NASDAQ. If we'd had venture capitalist investors, we wouldn't have bothered raising money after the first attempt at ten to twelve dollars per share came up short. Instead, they would have funded the company for another six months or year and then taken another run at the public markets when market conditions were more favorable and the company had shown even more progress. But we didn't have that luxury. I remember Dan Lufkin and Ken Langone, who supported me through the process, taking me out to lunch to talk about the deal. They told me that we never would have gotten it done if I hadn't taken the whole process personally and made it happen come hell or high water. Truth be told, nobody, including them, had thought we'd get the deal done at all. I thanked both for their support. I also thanked Dan for providing the insider participation, which he also did in several subsequent financings.

Guess what happened next? The fund that was so concerned that others would leave them holding the bag sold their entire position at seven dollars per share about six months later, for a forty percent profit. We later visited with them on a roadshow for a subsequent financing. On the night of pricing, I told the bankers not to let them have any influence on the deal. The result: they didn't participate. A few weeks later, I bumped into one of them on a street corner. He grabbed my arm and said, "You pulled off a nice deal." Should I have felt good about outplaying an experienced fund manager? Maybe. But I didn't. Instead, I felt angry and disillusioned. This was all a game to them. I'm not so naïve as to think that the investors in MELA were my friends, but after all we'd been dealing with at the FDA, it was exhausting to endure yet another powerful group of people who are ostensibly working *with* you but in reality have objectives that frequently diverge from your own.

My last dealing with that particular fund occurred three years after the IPO, when I happened to run into one of them at a banking conference. This guy was "good cop"— the one with whom I felt a good connection during the first IPO roadshow—but I hadn't run into him in subsequent visits to the fund. I asked him what the heck had happened to the investors who'd seemed to be sincerely interested in our company and its prospects. His reply? MELA had gone from being a promising investment to a really good "trading stock." What this meant was that there were enough shares trading hands each day and enough volatility (stock price moving up and down as a function of trading) in the stock that they were making money coming in and out of MELA on a regular basis. (And, obviously, participating in deals and then selling their position a short time later.) These guys were adding no value to the enterprise. They were taking minimal risk. They weren't developing a product that could save lives. No, they were subsisting off our work. There's a good half to Wall Street and a bad half. The good half helps finance promising ideas and also acts as the lubricant to the system. The bad half is nothing more than a leech attached to the real economy.

We did ten more financings for a total of $160 million in the public markets. Each of the financings took a great amount of work and were stressful. When you decide to go public, you are making a conscious decision to accept a whole set of other problems in exchange for access to capital. Small companies cannot handle being public as well as large companies. We had no other choice than to go public and accept the consequences, such as the market crash in 2007 and the manipulation that nefarious traders perpetrated during our battle with the FDA. MelaFind got on the market in the U.S. and Europe in 2012 because of all of the difficult decisions that we made and the great personal toll on me. As of the day I left the company in June 2013, I knew of sixty patients whose melanomas would not have been detected if MelaFind had not been used by their dermatologists—that's sixty lives saved. If we did not selflessly care, those melanomas would have been missed. That made it all worthwhile, and I would make all of those difficult decisions again to help those patients.

Change of Scenery

When our lease expired for the run-down office space in which the original team had started the company, as well as for two other non-contiguous suites, we had a tough decision to make. The choices were to have the landlord renovate the suites that we occupied and obtain options on additional contiguous suites, or take space in the Cosmopolitan Building, which was built in 1895 by Stanford White. The new location was across the railroad tracks from our current location. The landlord wanted us to move and he sweetened the deal—he said that he would give us twice the amount of space at one-half the current rate, and contribute fifty percent of the cost of the site renovation up to a certain amount. I wanted to move so that we could be in one location, which would greatly facilitate communication and comradery. Most of the employees, including the fundamental core team, did not want to move.

We worked with a local architect/interior designer named Sala, who knew the buildings well and was approved by the landlord. We designed a totally open floor plan that highlighted the historic section of the building with its large windows, huge steel fire doors, somewhat crumbling brick archways, and loft feel. The larger space in the back, which was added to the building in the 1950s was dark and used as a warehouse; we planned to open it completely to the historic space and install a great amount of lighting, so that from every angle a view out the front to the Hudson River would be seen—this would provide a sense that sunlight was shining into the whole facility. We were on a very tight budget, and we maximized that with styling and mood—few offices, few walls, mostly made of glass. We planned for a lunch room and small fitness center with shower facilities. We also provided for a large open space in the entry of the historic section so that we could hold our monthly company meetings.

We took the heads of all the departments to the facility once the prior tenants cleared out—it was totally bare, with nothing to show except its potential. Sala and I explained our thinking about the layout—I showed the department heads where I wanted to locate their respective teams, and why. One of the biggest reasons that I wanted to move was because we needed to incorporate FDA Quality System Regulation into every facet of what we do. We were in the most highly regulated industry—biotech and medical devices—quality is a critically important and mandatory function. The culture of the company was mostly Discovery, so formal quality processes, which are absolutely required by the FDA, European Commission, and other regulatory bodies for product approval and ongoing operations were not second nature, and they needed to be. We located the Quality Department in the middle of the company—the path to anywhere a person wanted to go (the cafeteria, bathrooms, accounting department, front door) was necessarily made to go through the Quality Department, which straddled the main walkway.

When it came to the Software and Algorithm team, I gave Nyq a choice—he could either have a large roomy area with a central area for collaboration or he could go in the back (next to the garage) and have his own door into the company since algorithm and software engineers typically worked very odd hours. I explained that the architect could do a number of things to the back to give it a Google feel—we already planned space for the ping pong table, pool table, and I provided my foosball table. Nyq was the most vocal opponent of the move. This was his first job—he came under the tutelage of the founding team and in ten years ascended to Project Team Leader and Vice President. He hated change. He often spoke in romantic terms about the "old days" and ridiculously cramped conditions under which he had to work—Nyq's height is 6′ 8″!

With disgust on his face he sneered, "Joseph, what does it matter where we go—it is all the same dark, depressing space." At first, I agreed with him—in its current state it was dark, but when you looked at the plans and heard the vision and listened to Sala, how could this be considered depressing? The problem that I had was that Dina and Nyq were the Secret Sauce and Key Ingredient—the fate of the company was totally dependent upon them. Dina did not want to move, but she worked from Princeton and came up to headquarters for certain meetings. But Nyq—he ate, drank, and slept at the company; the company was his family and his soul. He lived for two years in Germany to save the project during the re-engineering effort. He did anything and everything required to make the project successful. I also loved Nyq like a son (or little brother).

What was I to do? I woke up in the night quite upset. I knew that Nyq was being close-minded and childish. I also knew that he would love the new space once Sala's and my vision was made into reality. I met with Sala the next morning and I asked him, "Where is the darkest, dampest, dingiest, ugliest area of the whole space?" He took me to an area in the former warehouse below the loading dock—the building's septic cleanout pipe and all boiler pipes for the entire building went through the area; there were no windows. PERFECT, I thought.

I told Sala that I wanted him to make this the location of my office. He was aghast and tried to talk me out of it. My office was supposed to be in the turret of the historic part of the building—this was a semi-circular brick room with fifteen foot ceilings and twelve foot windows. It was bare, yet marvelously charming, and connoted gentle authority. Visiting analysts, investors, and partners would be sure to find it refreshingly different and intriguing; they would have an instantly favorable view of the company. I told Sala that it would become a small conference room for all departments.

Not only would my office be located in the least desirable place, it would be entirely glass. I wanted everyone in the company to not only to see what I was doing, but to also feel free and unafraid to approach me any time I was free. It was *en route* to the lunch room and bathrooms, and across the hall from the hardware engineers. The building's boiler pipes banged annoyingly every morning in the non-summer months to the point that I could not have phone calls or meetings in the office from 9:30 a.m.to 10:30 a.m. When the loading dock was used by large trucks, paint chips would fall from the ceiling onto my desk blotter, like dandruff on a blue suit.

I told Nyq what I was planning. He picked the larger open space rather than the space near the back entrance for his team. With his reluctant support, we moved forward and designed a fantastic space for our wonderful little company, which we grew to sixty-five full-time employees. The formal and chance encounters with members of the Quality department allowed for Quality ultimately to be integrated into every facet of the business.

As Alla, the first person hired for the Quality department said when I requested reflections for this book:

> You had an open-door policy and all employees knew that was for real. We were able to talk freely, ask questions, and discuss whatever we felt a need for; you understood importance of Quality Assurance/Regulatory Affairs and supported all department activities. You "empowered" my former department, constantly reminding all employees and requesting collaboration with QA. When we moved to the new offices, you decided to place the QA department in the center of the office, since QA is a 'heart of the company.'

Vivian Yost, our head of HR commented:

> Let's Build a Place That Sparks Innovation—MELA Sciences was growing and the employees were divided into two spaces. This contributed to silos in the organization and also contributed to a breakdown in communication between groups and people. Joseph saw this and moved the organization to a space that would allow us to not only work together, but more importantly build the culture he

knew was essential to the success of the organization. Thus, he made sure that the new space was full of light with glass, and not walls, to send a clear message that we were one team. His message was clear: "there will be no division or silos." Most importantly, Joseph placed his office right in the middle of the heart of the engineering and development areas, the "heart of the company." His office had walls made of glass so that there was no mystery around the CEO and he was accessible! "Actions always speak louder than words" and Joseph's actions drove not only synergy in the organization but a wonderful connection between Joseph and the staff. Most importantly, his actions drove the culture that was essential to the vision of MELA Sciences.

Let's Have a Party—Moving to this new space improved morale and teamwork. But Joseph knew that celebrating our accomplishments in this space was essential. So it was decided that the company holiday party would be in the new office. The whole company stopped early on a Friday afternoon to participate in decorating the office. The whole office was transformed into a magical space, with a Jazz band and wonderful food. Joseph knew that the budget was tight and he personally had a sushi bar set up that he financed. This was a wonderful team-building experience, but most importantly it gave the spouses and significant others the opportunity to experience the new space, and share the passion for what we were doing at MELA.

Personnel Decisions

Hiring is a process that vexes all organizations; this is especially true for small companies doing unprecedented things. How do you find qualified people, then determine whether they are a good fit, and introduce them to the company in a manner in which they will be successful? How can you determine whether a person with the right credentials and experiences is a good "fit," and whether his or her style will mesh well with the team? How do you know candidates are truly qualified? Even if you give them skills tests, which we did at MELA at all levels, you never can be sure. Are references really helpful, in other than severe outlier situations?

Once you've hired, several untoward things can happen—the skills you thought the person possessed aren't truly present, at least in so far as the application to your project. Or, the psycho-emotional make-up of the person does not mesh with the team. Or, the needs of the position change as the company grows and the person you hired is no longer suited for the job.

Inevitably, there come situations where a person must be let go—it pains me to say "fired," but so be it. I look at the decision to fire someone as the biggest failure of a manager. Unfortunately, I have had to fire a number of employees, and when I do, I examine how I failed in the hiring process or in managing the situation, and putting the new hire and the existing team within the right structure to succeed.

Selfless caring is not inconsistent with firing. I will argue that many managers do not fire enough people; rather they lateralize or implement structural changes so as not to have to release someone who really needs to be let go. Why? Because firing someone is a huge admission of failure; it is difficult, it is uncomfortable, and it does not make you feel good about yourself. When I was new to the industry, a poor performing peer was let go after a year of management refusing to see there was a problem and after another year of management trying to tell all of us there really wasn't a problem. When the person was finally fired I was sad for him and his family, but I felt good about the company—this meant that management could discern a good job from a poor one. It gave me faith in management and was inducement to continue to do the good work I was doing.

I carried that with me when I became management. I did two things—I acknowledged to employees who would complain about a poor performer that there is a problem, and I released employees who, no matter what was done—performance improvement plans, internal and external coaching, job shifting (if a suitable position was available), transfer to another department, etc.—could not be made to be productive assets to the company. The first behavior is critical—I know that it worked with me when I was young in my career, and I saw it work many times when I became a manager; being honest with employees, admitting that you see a problem, that you made a hiring mistake, goes a long way. I would even challenge the manager and peers of the bad performer to do things that could help make the person successful; sometimes it worked, most times it didn't, but, it always instilled confidence from the team that management was aware and was doing something to deal with the situation. If you selflessly care about the employees, you will do this. And, you will also part ways with someone when attempts at salvage have failed.

Another major challenge is dealing with managers who report to you and are very skilled at managing up, but are poor managers of their own departments. As the CEO, you should not have to spend much time managing. The people who report to you should be excellent managers and self-starting producers in their own right. And so you don't. And then what happens? You miss the signs of trouble. I have had this happen to me—a department head who reported to me was simply excellent in my dealings with him. No matter what time of day, night, or weekend and holiday, if I wrote a message to him, he'd respond faster than any other department head with exactly what I needed. I assumed that if he was this good and "on it" with my needs, he was naturally the same in his department. I assumed that the great understanding attitude and affable nature that he exhibited toward me was being, likewise, shown to his subordinates and peers.

Not so.

I realized there was a problem when I had a mutiny on my hands—the leaders of the department that he ran approached me, painting the picture of an unyielding intimidating tyrant with whom none of them could work. I validated this by speaking with other department heads, and HR also confirmed there was a problem. On the one hand, I was upset with myself that I didn't notice it sooner, because had I done so, I might have been able to intervene with coaching and more direct management. I was thrilled that the managers came to me without fearing reprisal—thrilled that they trusted me and didn't just "check-out" and resign one by one, as they found jobs. I believe that they came to me because I had built up a reservoir of good will with them. Still, I faulted myself for not having spotted this situation. Letting go of this person was my most difficult firing because he was very good in one aspect of his job (the one that I could see) but he could not change to become an effective manager, which was what the company needed from the position. I made a very difficult decision, which was greatly appreciated by many employees, and which deepened the reservoir of good will.

Another time, it became apparent that an employee named Bill needed to be fired. His manager, Amy, told me story after story of incompetence, and she did all of the right things—involved HR, put him on a performance improvement plan, provided additional direction—but nothing worked. One of the employees in the department, who was truly excellent, yet had a lesser title than Bill, was particularly upset; she outperformed him at every turn, yet made less. We had to let Bill go. This would be Amy's first firing, so I coached her and we role-played with HR to get her ready. I told her that I would be in the room with her when she did it. Once the meeting with Bill started, she couldn't do it; Amy got tongue tied and pale, so I took over and explained why, how, next steps, thanked him, and transferred him to HR. Amy was very embarrassed and was amazed at how quickly and unemotionally I did it, and she asked me how was I able to do it so easily. I told her that the key is to think ONLY about what is needed from the position that the person you are letting go has been inadequately filling. If you focus on the needs of the project, the company, and the other employees, when you have to do the most horrible deed, one that represents a manager's worst failure, you will be able to do it professionally and empathetically. I remember the look on Amy's face—when you make difficult decisions and do the dirty work, employees notice and greatly respect you.

CHAPTER 5

Set a Great Example

Charles Barkley, the "Round Mound of Rebound" (and one of my favorite basketball players), was known as a bad boy—brash, cocky, arrogant, and seemingly proud of his anti-establishment and counterculture positions and bravado. He was featured in a Nike commercial in which he said, "I am not a role model... Just because I can dunk a basketball doesn't mean I should raise your kids." To that I say, nonsense! Here is a man who achieved stardom and possessed a stage presence like few others. He had a tremendous opportunity to give to kids what they weren't receiving from their birth parents, which was parenting. And he didn't want it. In part, I believe that he didn't embrace the opportunity because he didn't want to be "on" all the time—he wanted to be able to relax, enjoy himself, and relieve himself of pressure, except when on the basketball court. That was his prerogative.

Many people don't want the responsibility of having to perform all the time. Managers and leaders are constantly under the microscope. While many accept that burden during work hours, or at least when they have to be visible to many people, they do not want it when their hair is down, so to speak. Yet, it is precisely during the unscripted and non-choreographed moments that leaders have their greatest impact. Stakeholders of all sorts, especially employees, can sense genuineness, and that is what motivates and rallies them. You are never more genuine than in the unrehearsed moments in life. Setting a great example is about putting yourself under the microscope and leading by example. It is hard work and it requires you to constantly be "on." Being CEO is a lonely job, and this particular behavior is a huge reason why.

Never Take No for an Answer

In 1998, I was the COO and an Executive Director of Anthra Pharmaceuticals, a specialty pharmaceutical company developing a drug for bladder cancer. The drug worked very well, achieving the endpoints in the clinical trial. We planned an IPO to raise money to launch the product with our partner, to develop additional approved uses of the drug Valstar, and to develop two other drugs in our portfolio for other cancers. The bankers thought it would be a great idea for us to undertake the IPO roadshow in Europe, and then come back to the U.S. (Maryland) to have the FDA Oncology Drug Advisory Committee (ODAC, or AdComm for short) meeting. After what would certainly be a positive outcome at the AdComm, the IPO roadshow in the U.S. would follow. Simultaneous with the AdComm meeting for Valstar was the American Urologic Association (AUA) meeting, which was taking place in San Diego; our marketing partner planned a big pre-launch meeting with its sales force at this event. After the AdComm, I was to fly across the country to San Diego to present at the pre-launch meeting and meet with Valstar investigators attending the AUA meeting, then fly back to N.Y. to commence the US IPO roadshow.

The amount of work involved in any one of these activities is considerable, and I was the main responsible party for the IPO and Advisory Committee meeting. In retrospect, it was absolutely insane to have these occurring simultaneously, but this was not my choice—we were a small company that was running out of money, beholden to opportunities to raise capital. The window (period of time that economic conditions are favorable for biotech companies to raise money via IPOs) for financing was getting narrower; we had to do it on this timetable. And so I had to perform. The fate of the company, its thirty-five employees, the product, and patients with refractory bladder cancer was on me.

I had prepared for these presentations like I had never prepared for anything before, and I am a preparer. I studied five hours per night in high school, college, and medical school, yet my wife, Adele, who had dated me since college, commented that she had never seen me prepare for anything the way I was prepping for the Valstar panel meeting. For several months before the AdComm, I attended and studied other AdComm meetings for cancer drugs. AdComm's are big, public spectacles, much like a trial, where the FDA is the prosecuting attorney and judge, the jurors are expert clinicians and other scientists from across the country, and you are the defendant. I was not impressed with the showings of the companies, their passionless, rote, and mundane presentations, their marginal grasp of their own data, or their inability to respond to questions facilely and effectively. The small companies were the worst—they had little to no credibility with the panel, and they looked like amateurs—frightened and small. At the last AdComm that I attended before ours, I got so close to the action that my left thigh was pressing against a corner of the U-shaped table arrangement at which the panel members sat—I actually leaned-in to the center of the discussion forum, peering at all parties involved, devouring what was being said, and studying their body language. I remember receiving dirty looks from the two panel members whose psychic space I was invading as I studied everything that was happening. I also remember showering the next morning and noticing a huge bruise on my thigh in that area—it hurt!

The next day, I told our team that we would deliver the best presentation ever given at an Oncology Drug Advisory Committee meeting—that was the goal, pure and simple. I told them that all of the presenters, from small companies, as well as large, look frightened and intimidated; they hide behind the podium, grabbing it like a shield when they are questioned. I told our team that I wasn't going to use the podium; rather I was going to stand in the middle of the U-shaped tables and walk around, engaging each of the panel members, looking them in the eye. I told them that there is no way on God's green earth that they could know the data better than I know it, and I want to communicate in word, action, and posture that this drug is great and needs to be approved now, not giving them the chance to possibly disagree! The employees and consultants looked at me as if I were possessed. Well, I was possessed. I told them that I won't be happy unless a panel member slaps the table and exclaims, "This is the way that we want all companies to present in the future." Janice Pruch, our medical writer and data presentation consultant, told me that she loved everything I said, except the part about not using the podium. I begrudgingly accepted her wise counsel and scrapped that idea.

Not only was I focused on the theater and dynamics of the AdComm meeting, I intensively labored through our complete data set at least five times—I told Adele that I had already mastered the data from the perspective of the way my mind works and I needed now to go through it from the perspectives of an oncologist, statistician, and regulator. I knew every fact. I made backup slides with the team and knew virtually all of them by number. Every person involved with the company—employees, consultants, clinical experts, directors, partners, and investors—saw what I was doing to make sure that we were successful.

There were three people on whom I relied unconditionally, and who witnessed everything—Janice, Denise Webber (head of clinical operations who ran the studies and the data entry/analysis team), and Al Thunberg. Janice is a literal genius who reminded me of my oldest sister, Mary. Janice is smart, measured, quiet, savvy, and wonderful. I listened to everything she said. Denise came with me to Anthra from Cytogen, where I felt she was the most underutilized resource. Denise is a former nuclear medicine technologist who ran clinical studies at a major hospital in Chicago. When she came to Cytogen, we were not working on the same projects, however her smarts and work ethic struck me. She still tells the story of a train ride to Washington, DC where I explained the way drug development and the FDA works, drawing on Amtrak Metroliner napkins for three hours. I think she still has the napkins! Al was from Sterling Pharmaceuticals—we were on opposite sides of a joint venture between our prior companies. He is a pre-clinical scientist who was pigeonholed at Sterling. He was smart, balanced, and whenever he spoke, his arguments made great sense. When I went to Anthra, I called Al and asked him to come aboard and head up pre-clinical and manufacturing, things he was not given the chance to do at his company. He was thrilled, and so was I.

Preparing for the AdComm and the IPO was ridiculously consuming. I was being bombarded from lawyers, bankers, board members, clinical investigators, and employees to the point of being unable keep up with all of the demands on my time. On one occasion, frazzled during a rehearsal with clinical experts and being called out of the room to attend to a matter with lawyers preparing the IPO documents, I whispered to Janice and Denise to make notes of everyone's feedback, but not to change any of the slides without telling me. I then told them to accept and incorporate whatever Al says, both today and going forward—that's how much I respected Al.

The IPO roadshow in Europe went very well—several investors indicated strong interest. Then, I headed to Maryland for the FDA showdown. I remember waking up the morning of the AdComm meeting: when I opened my laptop and saw the icons for the IPO roadshow and the AdComm meeting side by side on the desktop, I began to shake, which I found peculiar because I don't shake. I can still remember holding my hands out in front of me in disbelief watching them tremble. It was all coming down to this, the biggest moment of my career (up to that point). My parents were also attending this—they had no idea what I was doing with the M.D. degree for which they paid, and I figured watching their son go up against the FDA Oncology Drug Advisory Committee might disabuse them of their belief that I was wasting it, even though I had left my residency eight years earlier.

We made a fantastic presentation—we flawlessly and persuasively presented our case with confidence and humility. I sensed a real connection with the AdComm experts. Then, the FDA presented its case, basically against the product. During the FDA presentation, a senior FDA reviewer interrupted the presenter three times because erroneous data were contained on the slides and one slide that was shown should have been deleted altogether. The AdComm chair was not happy with this and asked me to come to the podium. This was highly unusual, but I did as I was asked to do—I went to the podium on our side of the room and looked at her awaiting a question. She looked at me and said, "Not that podium." I was stunned—the AdComm chair wanted me to go to the podium at which the FDA presenter was standing, on the other side of the room; this was unprecedented. I went over to the podium, smiled at the FDA presenter and felt awkward. The panel chair then asked me to present the FDA slides. If being at the FDA podium was unprecedented, presenting the FDA case against my own product was surreal! I advanced the slide, looked at what data were being displayed and the message that was being conveyed, and then presented it. At times, I did not agree with the point being made on the slide—I remember shaking my head, thinking to myself that I was in a *Twilight Zone* episode, and just continuing.

When I finished, the FDA asked questions, which I fielded first, then triaged to either our clinical expert, H. Barton Grossman of

MD Anderson Cancer Center; our statistical expert consultant, Mike Rubison; or the head of pre-clinical and manufacturing, Al Thunberg. This is where attending the prior six AdComm meetings and studying the dynamics really paid-off. I had noticed in the prior sessions that at some point, Dr. Robert Temple, one of the highest ranking officials at the FDA, takes over the meeting. In a Socratic manner, he steers the discussion where he wants it to go; by asking questions and noting the answers, he boxes-in the presenters from the company and obtains his desired outcome. His questions form an irrefutable logic-driven noose of rope made from your own words, then he fires a gun, the horse rides away, and you're left swinging from a sturdy branch. Your drug is toast and you go home in a body bag. I had seen it time and time again.

Dr. Temple asked me a few unrelated questions before starting to go down a certain logic path. He then started being Socrates; I knew what he was trying to do, so I beat him to it. I said, "Dr. Temple, I am going to save you from asking three more questions," then looked at Janice, who wrote all of the clinical reports and designed the slides with me, and said, "Slide number 113." Janice put it up; at first Dr. Temple continued to formulate his next question, using a downward arm motion with index finger pointed in my general direction. I remained silent. He looked at the slide and said, "That is exactly what I want."

He was trying to make the point that the compelling data on eradicating the disease would mean nothing if patients' cancers advanced shortly after therapy. So I showed him the relapse rate and stage of disease at relapse. He was satisfied. I was elated. After a few more easy questions from others that we addressed with aplomb, the morning session concluded.

At the intermission, I was mobbed from Directors, bankers, investors, employees and consultants. We were on cloud nine, for sure. Jim Quinn, one of our bankers, told me that he had never seen nor heard of anything like what just happened. No one had. We were prepared, we were relentless in our work, and we made outstanding formal presentations and impromptu responses. And, it was apparent to all 500 people in the room, including the FDA.

As I went to the men's room, perfect strangers blocked my path, grabbing me by the arm, telling me that what they just witnessed was amazing, and grinning, and shaking my hand. In the middle of all of this, I felt three taps on my back. It was the lead FDA reviewer on our NDA—let's call him Lance. He asked me whether I had a moment. I told him that he is the FDA, and for him I have an hour! Lance said it would take only a minute, then said, "Number one, that was a tremendous presentation—we wish all companies would present their data like that. Number two, you're an honest guy— you presented the bad equally with the good, and we noticed that. And, number three," he motioned me closer, and then whispered, "You've got it in the bag."

I then went to the bathroom, and came out to find our CEO and lead banker, and I told them what just happened. For sure, the U.S. leg of the IPO would be a victory party, and we would raise all the money we needed at the top of the price range. We just needed to sit through the afternoon, let the panel members debate things and go down ridiculous rabbit holes that meant nothing, grandstand a little, say things to be quoted in the media, and then finally vote positive on the approval. This would be a cakewalk.

The panel was reconvened. AdComm member after member had very supportive things to say. All was going well until an invited temporary panel member (Charles), who doesn't even treat patients with the stage of disease that the drug is intended to address, spoke up forcefully. He was playing devil's advocate by stating that we did not generate any data on survival. Well, our letter agreement with the FDA specified that efficacy would be defined by the complete response rate, which needed to be above 20%, and it was. We did not perform a survival study, and we were not claiming an increase in survival. Charles kept persisting. Mind you that his point is appropriate for drugs intended to treat late-stage cancer (that are seeking survival claims); however, it is completely inappropriate for early-stage bladder cancer. No other AdComm members were experts in bladder cancer. Charles finally said, "I don't care how good the data are; complete response is the completely wrong endpoint for this disease." He was dead wrong, but it didn't matter—he was from a very prestigious cancer center. It was the Johnnie Cochran moment. Whatever I said, nor, more importantly, what our expert, Dr. Grossman said, could reverse this. The panel voted 11 to 0 against approval of the product. Game over. Everyone packed-up. I was in shock and disbelief.

I rushed over to Lance and asked him what do we do next—the FDA is not bound by panel votes, and obviously they received erroneous feedback from someone who doesn't even treat the disease. Lance looked at me as if I were a stranger, not the guy he tapped on the shoulder four hours earlier, and said, "Joe, you heard the panel, it's done, and our decision is made." But, Lance, you just told me how great we did! It didn't matter; Lance was gone in a flash.

I got mobbed again, but not in a good way. Employees and consultants were looking for something positive from me, the bankers and lawyers had blood coming from their eyes, and the board was shocked, and asked me questions to which I could not respond without more research. The CEO, Michael Walker, shot me an encouraging smile, nod, and patted my arm; he did not smile often, so this was huge. Michael is a marketing and business development executive formerly from Merck—he has been to a few rodeos and he knows the risks when dealing with the FDA. Then my parents approached. My father offered to take me for a Scotch. I said that I couldn't because I had to run to the airport. With great consternation and concern, he said, "What could you possibly need to be doing right now that can't wait?" Distraught and lifeless I told him that there were more than 100 people in San Diego waiting to hear from me and, "I have to go be a leader now."

The flight from Washington National to San Diego was miserable—I was in the back of the plane with Denise. I cried the whole flight; no, I wailed the whole flight. It was the end of the world. I used the air-phone to call my old boss, Bob Maguire, the smartest guy in the industry that I know. I re-ran every moment in my head. By the time we landed, my eyes hurt, I had no voice, and I wasn't too steady on my feet. I got to the hotel, stared out my window, went to bed, woke up, and addressed our partner's sales team. This was not easy—I presented the data, informed them about Valstar presentations that would be made at the AUA meeting that they should attend, and told them that we would re-engage the FDA when I got home. I then met with a few of the clinical investigators who participated in the Valstar clinical trial. Dr. Grossman and I told them what happened. They were not shocked; they were angry, very angry. What happened at the AdComm demonstrated a complete lack of knowledge about *their* disease.

When I saw the anger immediately expressed by the first expert investigator, I realized that I was on to something. So I decided to get each subsequent expert with whom I met even angrier. We needed them to agree to help us with the next move, which had to come quickly, before the FDA sent us a rejection letter, which I am sure was being prepared. I knew that the ask was huge—who wants to be associated with a miserable failure, and 11-0 qualifies as exceedingly miserable. So I stoked their anger as well as their surgeon bravado. The biggest names in the program, several who were quite mild mannered, were not so mild, and agreed to help.

When I got back to New York, we had a meeting with the bankers. I remember them yelling at me. I have since learned in my career that bankers don't yell at you, you yell at them—but I didn't. Instead, I sat very calmly and unemotionally looking right past them and said that the FDA made a mistake and I was going to fix it. "Fix it? How the hell are you going to fix it?" I told them that I had called in the cavalry.

Regulatory counsel suggested that we file a supervisory review request with the FDA; this would stave off the rejection letter until such time as the agency adequately responded. We then requested a meeting with Dr. Bob Temple. We went down to the FDA a few weeks later and brought with us eleven urologist experts who performed the clinical trials—most in person, and a few via phone. The FDA had Charles participate by phone. It didn't take Dr. Temple long to figure out that a huge mistake had been made. He and I met privately right after the meeting, and spoke several times per week. We sent in some additional follow-up data from the patients in the study, as well as their medical histories prior to enrolling in the trial. A few weeks later, Dr. Temple called stating that we would be going back to the ODAC panel. Appearing at back-to-back panel meetings had never been done before. Moreover, challenging a panel rejection of this magnitude without a new study—heresy, right? It wasn't heresy because a mistake had obviously been made. But sometimes when people make a mistake, they don't want to admit it, especially in a public forum, so would the panel circle the wagons and be obstinate? I had to give the members a graceful way to elide from their previous erroneous position while at the same time communicating strength. These panel preparations were different than the first. I was angry because this work should not have been necessary. We should have consummated our IPO, launched the drug, and started clinical studies on other uses by now. (And, my parents should have come to the victorious one—they couldn't bear the thought of coming for *Rocky II*, so my brother came instead.)

Show time. The entire room was very, very tense. Everyone knew what happened just three months earlier. I rested my binder precariously on the top of the podium so that I could clear the shelf. The binder fell in front of the podium making a loud thumping sound, so I went around, picked it up, came back to the microphone, smiled, and said, "That did not happen in rehearsals." This was a great icebreaker—it centered me and communicated to the entire room and panel members that we were human, so we understand mistakes. The presentation went well—there was no drama this time. The FDA appropriately invited experts who treat the disease to participate; no doubt, this was enabled through meetings that Michael and I had been having inside the Beltway, informing all who would listen about the circumstances of the first panel meeting. Very short deliberations ensued, and we won the AdComm recommendation for approval by a vote of ten to one. Vindicated and victorious—we worked with the FDA on product labeling, and the drug was approved one month later.

The bankers sent me a case of Sterling Cabernet. But, there was no IPO. During the three months between the colossal mistake at the first panel meeting and the second meeting where we were victorious, the biotech financing window had shut. The company could not raise enough money to proceed. I left the company. The drug languished for a few years, then was acquired and launched. In 2013, Endo Pharmaceuticals reported net sales of $23.7 million, quite impressive fifteen years after its approval.

If many of us did not selflessly care, Valstar would never have been approved and would not have helped many patients. So often in business, as in life, the impossible is possible if those in a position to make a difference decide to make a difference come what may. Selflessly caring is also infectious—when the leader selflessly cares, others step-up their game and perform. I had not run AdComm meetings before my Valstar experience; I had not lobbied; I had not challenged the FDA; and I had not devised a strategy to reverse an eleven-to-zero debacle. But, I had always selflessly cared at everything I did. I threw a lot against the wall to see what would stick—a lot didn't (like my idea of not using the podium). Sometimes, you have to admit it was a bad idea and go back to the drawing board. If you selflessly care, you keep at it and you don't take no for an answer and you are not vested in your own ideas.

I asked Al Thunberg, to comment on the premise of selfless caring as a business strategy for this book:

You surprised me once, when I joined the company, when you told me I would be doing CMC and preclinical for the Valstar NDA (New Drug Application), whereas Michael had hired me to transition the next product from preclinical research to clinical development. It was quite a charge! I appreciate the opportunity, and I'm glad I was able to deliver.

What I remember most about you was your commitment and your determination. This was on display throughout the NDA process. You became famous for refusing to take "no" as the FDA's answer to the Valstar NDA, but this was just a (somewhat extreme, perhaps) extension of your approach to pharmaceutical management. You taught me to find a way around all obstacles, and I thrived under your leadership. You listened, gave good direction, gave me enough rope to hang myself, and supported my decisions. This was unique in my working experience, so I applaud you for your supportive, non-confrontational approach to management. I should add that you probably figured out early that I do not like to be managed. More credit to you for making our relationship work!

Al's last point is important—he is older than I am, worked in a big company environment, had a lot of experience, and we have very different personalities. We were once discussing a difficult situation with some old data that had been generated before we joined the company and I asked a non-sequitur rhetorical question, not anticipating a response— "Why, why do you think this keeps happening?" Al is very quiet, pensive, and considers everything he is thinking of saying five times before saying it. He snapped, and in an animated tone said, "Because you are a raging extrovert, and I am an introvert!" Message delivered. Technically, in the ways of hierarchical management, I was his "boss," and he just challenged me, right? Nonsense! I NEVER say that I am anyone's boss—I say that we work together. And, if we are going to work together and be successful, I can't put myself first. No, I have to selflessly care enough to focus on the issue and work the problem. I found a way (after trying several options) to work with him and make him feel good about working with me. And, we clearly made it succeed.

The Company Meeting and Breakfast Meetings

By far, the monthly company meeting was my most effective, therefore favorite, management and leadership tool. We assembled the entire company at eleven a.m. for one hour, followed by a lunch (alternating between pizza and Chinese food). The management committee (MC), which was composed of all of the department heads, would meet first from 9:30 a.m. to 11 a.m. During the MC, I would update the managers on the major external and cross-functional things affecting the company, as well as the rationale behind requests and decisions that were made. Projects and issues that crossed-over between departments would be discussed amongst the department heads. I would review with the MC the theme of the comments that I would be making at the company meeting and ask the members for input. I also asked them to share with each other highlights of the major activities going on in their departments. Last, we would vote on the nominations for MELA Awards (see Chapter 3).

We would then proceed to the company meeting, where all employees would assemble near the front door in the lobby, an area we designed specifically for these sessions. As the first order of every meeting, I would discuss the positive events that happened this month, as well as the bad things. Questions could be asked at any time, and I constantly called on people while I spoke to prompt them with questions that would help me make my case. I would drop hints as to the theme of the unifying comments that would be shared at the end. We would then deal with the perfunctory issues—stock trading windows, enrollment in health plans, employee training delinquencies, warnings about stealing toilet paper, etc. Then, each manager would speak for five to seven minutes to highlight to the entire company important projects and acknowledge key contributions. Next, managers introduced new employees who then had to briefly speak about themselves. The MELA Award would be handed-out—the person who nominated the award winner would read the application that had been submitted and then hand the award to the winner. Finally, I would summarize the meeting while explaining a unifying insight and continuing to interact and ask questions of the employees.

My themes would match the accomplishments and cadence and tenor of the month's activities. Many times I had what I thought were excellent and witty ideas based on news and sporting events, or TV shows or movies, earlier in the month that could not be used because they did not fit the message that was needed to be delivered. I frequently completely scrapped my ideas, and developed a new one on the train ride to the company.

Storytelling is good—people like it when the leader shares bits about himself in an unscripted manner. But storytelling is only useful to the company and the employees if it addresses an issue that needs addressing. When you are the CEO, employees look to you to talk; however, I never wanted to talk for the sake of talking, or in order to satisfy some personal need. So I thought long and hard about these meetings, about melding the most important events of the month by a unifying theme that would achieve something. I am a believer of positive reinforcement and of inspiring employees. But sometimes, the conditions on the ground warranted other less uplifting messages in order to challenge employees to do better.

I always had notes in my hand during the company meeting, and I also took notes during it as managers would speak or employees would ask me questions or raise points. I did this to show my colleagues that I cared enough about them to have prepared seriously and that I did not want to omit anything. I wanted them to know that these meetings meant a lot to me. Employees model the leader's behavior—if I didn't take the meetings seriously, nor would they. If I didn't prepare, why should they prepare? And that is why I loved the company meetings and felt they were one of my best tools as leader. The employees saw the example that I set in my preparation, my respect for the managers, my acknowledgment of them, my joy in their successes, and the seriousness with which I took my job and theirs.

Often, too, in the middle of my ending summary and discussion, I did not get the answer that I was hoping to get from the questions that I would ask of employees. If I couldn't handle the tangent in the moment, I would write it down, finish my thought, and then address the point. Implementing the company meeting in this way left me exposed, and I liked the message that sent to employees, as well. It is okay to put yourself at risk, to be vulnerable, as long as you are honest.

No question was off-limits. I know that a lot of managers and executives say that until an employee asks a difficult, if not gotcha, question. But, I never shied away from them, and employees felt comfortable enough with me, and trusted me enough, to ask these questions, both publicly at the company meetings, and privately. I viewed employee questions as opportunities to inform the team about the myriad of issues that must be considered. I had the opportunity of seeing, and being buffeted with, all of the factors; they did not. I can't remember a time when I explained the panoply of forces at work and broader context that I wasn't able to address and diffuse a tough or tense situation. I cared enough about them, and respected them enough, to believe that given the same information that I had, they would at least see the wisdom of the decision or the magnitude of the challenge.

As Vivian, our head of HR pointed out:

Always say "why" first then give the answer—I was always struck by the manner in which Joseph responded to requests or questions. He always gave the "why" first and then the answer or information. This is profoundly important as Joseph knows an effective CEO gains understanding first to pave the way for acceptance. A great example of this took place during a company meeting when an employee questioned "why" don't we just do "x." This employee was clearly frustrated with the path Joseph had chosen for the organization is response to the FDA. Joseph could have just said "no, that won't get us where we need to be." Joseph knew that once an employee hears "no" he then has to set about defending his point. Of course, the employee may or may not buy into Joseph's explanation after already hearing "no." Joseph's methodology of always educating first, then giving the answer (which is obvious at the end of the education process) brilliantly gains respect and acceptance.

Every year on the first Monday of May, we would have a company meeting in Times Square, New York, at the NASDAQ Stock Exchange. MELA Sciences was invited to ring the opening bell on Melanoma Monday, a national day of awareness of the dangers of melanoma skin cancer. I decided that rather than a few of us going—most companies have just the CEO and CFO or other officer—we would bring the entire company. The last time we did it before I left there were sixty-five employees huddled around the podium, pushing the button, having their faces shown on a huge Jumbotron screen and on cable business shows. The employees loved participating and seeing the skin cancer screenings that we sponsored and meeting patients for whom the product that we were developing would be helping. As Vivian states:

"Why are we doing this?" Joseph would take every opportunity to reinforce the message of "why" we do what we do at MELA. This one important factor is what made the difference between "working for MELA Sciences" and "believing in and being committed to what you and the organization do every day." This may sound trite, but it was what made the difference between employees performing their jobs in an acceptable manner, versus truly caring and having passion for their jobs. This was best exemplified by Joseph taking the whole company to the NASDAQ stock exchange on Melanoma Monday, to ring the opening bell. The employees would participate in the ceremony and hear an important message about Melanoma and our mission to save lives. It was truly exciting and yet humbling as one year as he invited two patients with melanoma (one who subsequently did not survive and another who did survive). The story of what we do and "why" we do it was profound as we met these patients and heard their stories.

Invariably during the company meetings there were employees who were simply not "buying what I was selling," so to speak. I would write that down in my notes as well, and then follow up with them later to see what was on their minds. Sometimes, my main inspiring theme did not inspire some—that actually happened more than a few times with the software and algorithm team. This was a tough group, and I would need to meet directly with them and explain myself in terms that resonated with them.

During an MC meeting prior to an employee meeting, I said to the department heads that I just wasn't feeling well and invited any of the leaders to run the meeting for me that day. I was ill and I was mentally and psychologically beaten. Although I had prepared for the meeting, as usual, I lost my mojo, so to speak. I did not feel inspired—what I had prepared to discuss was not even resonating with ME, so how could I expect it to inspire anyone? If you are no longer passionate about something, then no one will be passionate about what you're saying. Your words will sound contrived and artificial. To avoid that circumstance, I figured that having one of the department heads run the meeting would be a nice change of pace that would be received well by the employees. I was hoping that several of them would volunteer, but nobody did. I looked around the table and my eyes landed on Jeff, the head of R&D. He said, "No, you gotta do it because we need to hear the things you say." He used the word "we," not "the employees." He also said that the company needed my inspiration. I agreed but said I needed to end the MC meeting early in order to think about a theme that inspired me so that I could be inspirational. So I did. Funny, it seemed to be a very good one—in fact, Vivian told me it was among the best messages that I ever delivered. This experience reinforced several things:

1. When you are the leader, you gotta lead, no excuses;
2. Authenticity is critical and more important for leadership than the content, itself—I did not have enough time to develop great content, so I focused on what was real to me in the moment, and it was very well embraced;
3. Employees truly loved these meetings and they were the best way to align and mobilize the entire team around the common goal(s).

As Diana commented:

He was great at getting the company focused and aligned from the standpoint of getting everyone on the same page with where the Company was headed and how to get there.

Well, the monthly company meeting was the way I did that.

Delegate, but Audit

Many managers have difficulty learning how to delegate and then trusting that others can do the job that they, themselves, have done and can do very, very well. It is important to trust, but then you need to verify. What happens when the tasks you are delegating affect the culture of the company? I observed at MELA that some department heads did not convey values that I felt were critical, or they did not live them to the level that I felt necessary. My values and the behaviors that I wanted modeled and reinforced seemed not to be getting through. We had to change that.

I started having weekly breakfast meetings with every department on a rolling basis. This was a great way for me to reinforce the values and behaviors that I held so dearly and that were front and center at the company meetings. Employees leave jobs because of their managers and I wanted every employee to feel that they had some real connection to me; making myself more available to them in the day-to-day matters established that contact. The breakfasts turned out to be a great idea for another reason—the managers used them as a means of recognizing and rewarding their great performers; these employees got a chance to present and explain what they were doing in much more detail than could be done at the company meetings. Here is another example of a tactic performed out of selfless caring that paid great dividends not only for the issue it was attempting to address, but in another very important way.

The Company Softball Game

MELA Sciences was a collection of very unique people. One day, I looked around and realized that we had at least one person from every continent and every major religion on staff. We were our own little United Nations. The "Ugly American" that I am, I decided to have a company softball game and cookout. It was an utter debacle. Three quarters of the employees had never held a baseball bat in their hands. The Indian guys thought we were playing cricket and ran to first base holding the bat. The European contingent wanted five strikes, not three. Baseball mitts were on the wrong hands. Some people threw the ball at the runners, not the base to which they were running. It was like a scene out of *The Bad News Bears*.

One of our electrical engineers who had just come back earlier in the week from recovering from a heart attack, tried to stretch a single into a double. As he was rounding first base, running hard to second base, eyes wide open and fixated on the goal, he tripped and did a belly-flop. Even though the infield was made of sandy clay and it was a dry day, he did not slide, rather all that momentum (he is portly) just stopped as he struck the ground with a mighty thud. Bloodied chin and knees and elbows, he crawled to second base. All of us were stunned, on tenterhooks just staring at him waiting for him to collapse, praying and hoping that he did not have chest pain or another heart attack. He was fine and, thrilled that he was safe; not medically, rather that he was safe at second base! This game had it all. Little did I know that it made an everlasting impact on everyone. We did it only once, but they still talk about it to this day, as evidenced in Alexei's comment in Chapter 3.

On the evening of the MelaFind AdComm panel meeting when nothing at all was going right and we had just received notice of shareholder lawsuit solicitation, things managed to quiet down, just a bit. The second day of the preparation session, which turned into a free-for-all for hours, had miraculously abated to just a low din. Literally, for the first time all afternoon, I was able to sit down by myself. I put my face in my hands as I leaned forward in the chair, elbows on knees. I closed my eyes tightly, let out a low groan and sighed. I wanted just a few moments to meditate to myself as I was faced with many more hours of work to do with Dina, Kathy, and Leela after our experts would go to their rooms. It felt good to be alone in my own little world, in the middle of a crowded room, albeit for just a very brief time.

After about a minute in this state, I felt a tapping on my shoulder. I was startled and jumped out of the position to see our head of IT, who said, "I saw that you had a free moment, and I thought it would be a good time to give you this." It was roughly a foot and a half by two feet long, wrapped in white paper. He said that he had been telling the team back at headquarters what was happening and all that I was going through, and they wanted me to have this, from them, so that I knew they were thinking of me. It was a picture from the company softball game, signed by all the employees who were back at the office and those with me in Maryland at the panel meeting. I burst out in tears—our head of IT felt terrible saying that he had hoped it would make me smile. Well, for starters, I was having five crying spells per day at the time. Second, the magnitude of the situation hit me like a ton of bricks—fifty jobs were riding on the outcome of this AdComm panel, and it was not going well, at all, and I was responsible.

I chuckled to myself as it was reminiscent of the scene in *My Cousin Vinny* when Vinny Gambini (Joe Pesci) was feverishly preparing for the murder trial of his cousin and Mona Lisa Vito (Marissa Tomei) decided to engage him about their future together as a couple. The signed softball poster was akin to Lisa's biological clock going tick, tick, tick. I identified with Vinny in that moment—with the fate of the company, patients with melanoma, a shareholder lawsuit, and my career riding on the outcome of this trial, I did not need additional importance piled on top! All I could think of was them, as well as the patients and investors, who also had a tremendous amount riding on the outcome of this case, if you will. And, they thought about me and wanted to show their support to me. It was a wonderful moment and one that only occurred because of selfless caring.

In the Unsuspecting Moments

You, as the leader, are scrutinized at every moment; employees are looking all the time at what you are doing. You are setting an example every second, whether or not you intend to do so. I reminded myself of that and challenged myself to always set a good example by placing my office where it was (under the loading dock) and making it entirely glass so that employees could see when I arrived and left, and what I was doing, which wasn't practicing putting!

I once told Jenna very early in her time with me that she needed to keep her eyes and ears open and observe everyone and everything and to make notes about people and how they behave. I told her that she would soon have seen enough different situations (in the office in good times and bad times, on the road, at meetings, etc.) to begin to construct the ideal person whom she wants to be. I told her that in real life, no one is perfect, so you can't model any particular

123

individual. Instead, you strive to model positive behaviors, and avoid negative ones. I told her that it was my hope there were more behaviors that I exhibited that she endeavored to emulate than those she would vow never to follow. But, I told her, there will be things that I would do that would fall on the negative side of the ledger.

Still, I constantly tried to do things that would be positively modeled. The original working title of this book was the *24 Hour Manager* because I firmly believe that being a successful manger and leader means that your job, employees, and shareholders need to be on your mind twenty-four hours a day; inspiration comes at odd times and when we come at things from different angles under different circumstances, we tend to obtain our most business-enabling insights. The same is true for setting a great example—you need to do it ALL THE TIME because you never know when you are being watched and, therefore, when you have the opportunity to inspire and lead by example.

Intensity and Perseverance

Part of setting a great example is never asking anyone to do things that you wouldn't do, and I didn't. What's more important is that people noticed, and emulated the behaviors. I would wash dishes that piled-up in the sink, make coffee, empty trash from the kitchen containers that had garbage overflowing onto the floors, clean the conference room after meetings, and replace light bulbs. Once, a senior manager emerged from the bathroom complaining quite graphically about the condition in which the toilet bowl was left by a prior user; he went to Vivian (our head of HR), to me, and as many others as would listen. I took a look; it was bad, really bad, so I cleaned it. Problem solved. To me, if something was out of place or not right anywhere in the company, it was my responsibility, and if I could fix it, I would. This established an ownership culture that many others, but not all, adopted.

Once MelaFind was on the market, we hired at a more rapid rate, so new employees did not have the benefit of fully appreciating and participating in how we ran the company as much as employees who had been with us for a few years. We were installing several MelaFind systems at a dermatology practice in Houston, Texas. I was onsite for the training and installation procedures and to meet with the lead dermatologist, who was a skin cancer expert. I got there early, met the delivery team and helped to unload the systems and de-crate them, in my suit and tie. A new employee commented to me that he could not believe that the CEO was doing this kind of job. I explained to him that this is what we do at MELA—if there is a void, we expect all employees to fill it, no matter what it is. I also took the opportunity to explain how his job is every bit as important as my job, especially his role in satisfying the customer. He took a deep breath and smiled, so proud of himself, as well he should be. He told the story to the other installers at the next company meeting. One time, I did this at a trade show and I got a really bad splinter as I reached into the crate blindly. I found a dermatologist to carve it out of me and stitch my skin. When I was back at the office, I spoke to our head mechanical engineer who designed the crates and told him to sand and paint the interior surfaces because I did not want the guys who do this routinely getting hurt; he redesigned the crate. I cared selflessly and I did many things that employees normally did so that I experienced the things with which they were dealing, and I addressed problems, proactively, not waiting for complaints.

We raised $160 million in the public markets, an extraordinarily difficult feat in medical technology. We did it in eleven separate transactions over eight years. I wasn't just selling stock in MELA, or its great product, MelaFind. No, I was selling myself. I was continually meeting with investors; I took each meeting seriously, expending great energy in preparation and in delivery of the story. I was explaining to our CFO that this is the way I want the company perceived. He looked at me quizzically, so I said to him, "What is the one word you would use to describe me." He did not hesitate for a second, saying, "Intensity," I said, "Exactly! That is just what I want investors, potential investors, doctors, nurses, and patients concluding about our company." When you are intense, you exhibit passion, for sure. But, people also conclude something else—you will be undeterred in achieving your goal. I projected that intensity outside of the company and inside the company. Everything was important to me; everything mattered; everything had to be done right. I demanded that of myself, and I demanded it from employees. Often, I fell short and they fell short, but we quickly corrected, tried again, and never lost our resolve.

On the morning that we announced the FDA approval of MelaFind, after years of difficulty and public fighting with the FDA, I received an email from our lead investor entitled, "Perseverance." In it, he congratulated me for never giving up, expressed his amazement at our achievement against all odds, and he said that the following was his father's favorite quote:

> Nothing in the world can take the place of persistence. Talent will not; nothing is more common than unsuccessful men with talent. Genius will not; unrewarded genius is almost a proverb. Education will not; the world is full of educated derelicts. Persistence and determination alone are omnipotent. (Calvin Coolidge)

Employees will follow a leader who demonstrates the skill and ability, along with the desire, to win. They will follow the example set by you.

"Caretensity"

This is a word that I just made up, but it fully captures what I am trying to convey in this book. A person who is described as "caretensive" makes whatever he is doing in that moment the most important thing in the world to him. A caretensive person feels if it is important enough to do, it is important enough to do well. An uber-caretensive person does his absolute best at everything he attempts and defines his work product as himself.

I have been uber-caretensive for as far back as I can remember. Whether it was in waxing and detailing the cars of all the drivers in my family—I am the youngest of four children, so I could never just wash my car; I had to wash everyone's car. Also, I couldn't do mine any better than the others', so if I wanted my car to look spectacular for a date with Adele, I had to do the five others with that same level of care and results.

My after-school and summer job in the late 70s and early 80s was maintaining the high school that I attended. I was the only student on the crew who repaired and installed things (plumbing, electricity, ceiling tiles, etc.), painted, and landscaped. I worked with two older men (Jimmy and Rich) who were retired tradesmen. Other students, approximately a dozen, worked on the cleaning crew. One day over the summer the police met with Rich and told him that there were many complaints of vandalism in the town, so they recommended that we either cut down the beautiful row of pine trees that encircled the front and sides of the school, or we trim the bottoms so that the police could see potential vandals from the street.

So I spent the whole day cutting the branches of the pine trees at the tree trunks with a hand saw up to four feet off the ground. This was hard work—I filled many trailer loads and took them in the tractor (it was fun driving the tractor) to the dump, repeatedly. I finished the whole job in one day—more than forty trees, six to eight boughs per tree. I was exhausted, achy, blistered, scratched and scraped, dirty, full of sap, and smelling like Pine-Sol. As I was driving out of the parking lot in the front of the school, from a distance I noticed that it looked horrible—uneven with variable heights from ground to first bough for every tree. How could this be—I measured each one! I realized that I did not account for the weight of the boughs— the longer and heavier boughs drooped. I measured each tree at the trunk, not at the periphery.

127

Rich saw me looking at it from the street and got out of his car. He told me that we'd fix it in the morning, smiled, and drove off to go home. Not me; no way. This looked terrible and I wasn't going to let it stand, even for just one night. Sisters and Brothers lived at the school— I wouldn't want my home looking like a drunk amateur did work in the front of it, so why should they have to experience this? Who knew whether they would be having visitors, perhaps out of town family or colleagues, who would not likely be coming back soon, if at all? So I got the tractor, trailer, and saw and had at it for another few hours, looking from the street after each fine tuning, until it was perfect. I drove away looking at it, smiling with great pride. To this day, thirty-five years later, the school still has those trees, which are now very tall and full. But, the first four feet are pruned uniformly making the front of the building visible from the street. I grin every time I drive past.

I told the story earlier in the chapter about how I prepared for the Valstar AdComm panel and my goal of eliciting a table slap and declaration from a panel member that ours was to be the new standard of how every company should present. Was this a BHAG (big hairy audacious goal, care of James Collins in *Built to Last*)? No, this was caretensity! If I were doing it, it had to be the best.

I operated this way in executing my work tasks, and in managing people. I would continually do the two things that we talked about in the introduction—doggedly prepare, as well as apply myself empirically trying and erring, and trying again until we got it right. And, I would persist and persevere, no matter what, until the objectives were achieved.

In medical school, I was having a lighthearted argument with one of my anatomy lab partners who was teasing me a bit about something over which I was perseverating. Bill was endeavoring to become an orthopedic surgeon and I wanted to be an internist (Hugh Laurie's *Dr. House*, but without the sex and Vicodin addictions). If it didn't involve a bone or a joint, he didn't very much care about it. I told him it was important to me, and he just nodded his head and smirked while I stressed myself over something trivial to him. I looked at him and said, "Whether you care to admit it now or not, this is exactly why you are going to send your mother to me." He smiled and said, "You know Gulfo, I hate to tell you this, but that's right, I am going to send my mother to you." Caretensity.

Traveling is No Excuse

Often in my career, I needed to travel over weekends. Although Catholics are given dispensation if they cannot attend Sunday Mass due to travel, I would never miss it; it was interesting to go the church in different cities. At MELA, Jenna and Diana would go with me. One Sunday, upon hearing the Gospel, I realized that Jesus had a formula—whenever someone approached him with a problem, he seemingly always did the same three things:

1. Assured the individual that they were in a safe place next to Him by wishing them peace;
2. Addressed a particular need or problem presented by the individual;
3. Challenged them to do something, usually to live a life more in keeping with their potential.

I said in the introduction that Jesus is the greatest manager and leader that the world has ever known. Indeed! His truly is the winning formula when an employee comes to you with a problem:

1. Let them know we are in this together and somehow, someway we will come out of it;
2. Help them to correct a situation and teach them what went wrong;
3. Express your confidence in them by challenging them to do better.

What an example!

CHAPTER 6

Take Chances on People & Cultivate Talent

This may sound counter-intuitive, but if you selflessly care about the company, you need to take risks. Of course, taking chances on people is usually great for them, but may appear risky for the company and the shareholders. Think again. If you selflessly care, you will realize at some point that the best dynamics and greatest insights come when people are challenged to do more than they think they can accomplish. Of course, the chances are calculated, but chances nonetheless. My brother, Vin, tells a great story about when he was in the second year of his surgery residency—at the start of a gall bladder removal, before the first incision was made, the lead surgeon handed him the scalpel. This is not typically done until a student's fourth or fifth year. In year one, the resident holds retractors while in year two, the resident may tie off an artery or snip something that the surgeon is holding. Making the opening incision, well, that is quite advanced. Vin told me he hesitated, trembled, and looked at the surgeon who said to him, "Don't worry, there is nothing you can ____-up that I can't fix." He stopped trembling and proceeded.

When you are leading a small company, it isn't quite like that. After all, you don't have the time to shadow everyone to fix problems. But, it is important to let the team know that together, we can fix any damaging outcome that follows from their decision-making and execution if we know about it early enough. You also have to let them know that you trust them, that we will deal with the consequences, and that you are confident that the good will dwarf the bad. When I was running MELA Sciences, I had seven direct reports. By the time you are reporting to the CEO, you had better be highly experienced, require little direction, be in control of your emotions, and be an excellent manager. Well, in a little company, not so much. So, as CEO, I had to supplement the talent more so than Ian Read at Pfizer would need to do, for sure. I had enough time and energy to handle just one "project," that is, a manager who required a lot of co-managing. This one person was Leela.

Uncut Diamonds

Leela is the most unique person that I know. She came to the company after graduating from Wesleyan. She was working part-time in a bookstore when she answered an ad to join the clinical group as a research assistant. Seven years later, she was Director of the department reporting to the CEO (me) with four direct reports and a handful of consultants reporting to her. Leela is benevolently irreverent and countercultural. Every topic, no matter how embarrassing, is fair game for humor or ridicule. There is no rule that she doesn't feel comfortable challenging. And, she is very passionate. I felt like the Reverend Mother to her Maria in *The Sound of Music*—she could throw a whirling dervish out of whirl. And, she'd rather be playing a guitar and singing on stage than doing anything else. At MELA, I quickly became very accepting of people who don't fit molds—I found most geniuses and very gifted people are like this, and I wanted to retain, attract, and engage the most creative and insightful people available, so I had to learn how to do it. I received the equivalent of a PhD learning how by working with Leela!

In her early years at the company, I would show her things in much the same way as I would show Alexei. I have a lot of experience in the industry in clinical and regulatory, so it was natural that I spent a lot more time with the clinical department and Leela than with Alexei. When it came time to file with the FDA an Expedited Review application for MelaFind, I had asked Leela's boss, Kathy, to do it, but she said she was too busy. Fair enough. I could have written it in a half day having drafted successful Expedited Review applications previously. But, I wanted someone in Clinical to have this experience for several reasons. First, I wanted it on someone else's cv—it is a great deliverable to have achieved and my cv already had it. Second, it would help them get a better handle on the project, as a whole, which is important when speaking to investigators and in preparing the final approval dossier.

Leela was very excited at the opportunity, but also frightened. I sat with her and explained the procedure, as per FDA regulations. There are six possible criteria—being judged by the FDA to have successfully satisfied just one of the six is sufficient to receive the designation. Step one was for Leela to explain whether and how MelaFind met each of the possible criteria. We met to discuss her thoughts and I shared mine, as well. Leela prepared a full draft, complete with data. I also had her write the cover letter to the FDA, which I edited. We sent it in, and the FDA awarded MelaFind Expedited Review based on three criteria—wow! She did it, in just her second year on the job, and she felt great about it.

I had to learn to deal with quite a bit in managing Leela, along with a few other young employees. You see, the concept of in-the-office work hours were anathema to Leela and her boss, Kathy—Leela came into the office in the morning whenever she wanted, usually around 11 a.m. She would leave late, as well. Or, sometimes she would leave with everyone else, but then I would get emails and reports from her between 3 a.m. and 6 a.m. As Vivian Yost, our Director of HR told me, Leela is a Millennial and they view their lives as a mosaic—they multitask constantly. Millennials do not compartmentalize their lives—work, recreation, family, and personal—nope, it is all one big happy bag of Chex Mix, all the time. I tried to explain that being in the office for designated times was not about face time, or *Mad Men*-era vestiges, rather it was important for work. She would often tell me that she would get more done at home. Yes, I do too, but it isn't just about getting work done, it is about the interplay between people. She wasn't buying it, and did not subscribe to it.

I allowed her to work this way for many reasons:

1. She produced work of great quality and quantity.
2. She had tremendous potential.
3. She was a favorite personality in the company and could get others to give her whatever she needed in order to complete her tasks.
4. She was very creative and I know that creativity happens at different times and under different circumstances for different people.
5. I felt it was a maturity issue that would resolve itself soon.
6. Letting her work as she wanted brought her closer to me and allowed me to have a greater impact on her—exerting positional authority and demanding that she work in a manner she did not want would have driven her away.

I was able to adapt my manner of working and adjust to the way she and Kathy, Leela's manager, and Nyq liked to work. It made my job harder, but I felt the rewards were worth the effort. So I allowed it, and we flourished. Leela and I also became very close. I felt that I was having an influence on many facets of her life, and that was very important to me because I cared about her, a lot.

I wasn't that great a guy, however—some of our work had to be done a certain way, notably, visiting the hospitals and clinics where we were performing our clinical studies. Leela and Kathy did not like to travel. Neither did I; however, nothing beats face-to-face contact with people in their offices. I say this admitting that I used to need three Scotches to get on an airplane and a few more (depending on the length of the flight and amount of turbulence) in the air! I dreaded travel, but I had to do it frequently because the results from in-person meetings far exceed the outcomes of telephone calls and emails.

I remember once needing to get to Chicago for an early morning meeting on a Monday, but I did not want to leave Adele on Sunday evening. So I took a 6:30 a.m. flight from Newark Airport. When I got to the airport, no bars were open! I got on the plane frightened for my life; I gripped the armrests so hard that my knuckles were white. I grimaced, prayed, and held my breath during take-off. Once in the air, I anxiously waited for the flight attendant who was making rounds with two carafes in her hands asking passengers whether they wanted coffee or juice. When she got to me, I nodded no and then motioned her closer. I whispered, "Do you have any Scotch?" Startled, she said yes with a very quizzical look. I then said I would take three bottles with ice in one glass. She nodded, turned and kept pushing the coffee and juice on other passengers. As she returned to the galley, a dozen rows ahead of me, she called back, "Sir, will that be Dewar's or Chivas?" Everyone within earshot turned to look at the lush, meaning me. I meekly replied that Dewar's was fine and kept my head low. For years, I needed to pre-medicate myself or at least have alcohol at the ready in case of turbulence.

I explained to Leela that I learned early in my career that when I visited doctors in their office they became friends for life! Seriously, when you visit a clinical site, meet the staff, break bread with them, discuss issues, offer solutions, and bond with them, they perform at a very high level. Of course, study sites need to be visited to check on data quality, however I wanted the sites visited much more often than for quality purposes. We were conducting the largest study ever performed in melanoma, and we needed to complete it quickly, so accrual into the study was a huge issue. Leela and Kathy resisted leaving the office, and I forced the issue because it was critical to the project. They still did not go as often as I would have liked so I visited the sites myself. This actually was an excellent thing to do because I learned a great deal from the melanoma experts when I visited, and often used the information and insights in presentations and discussions. The rapport and mutual respect that was built with them came in very handy when we had to fight with the FDA.

The lightbulb did finally go on, as Leela commented on these two topics:

Face time yo!! Wow, that was a big illogical learning. Forty-eight hours spent traveling to deliver Subway sandwiches to a clinical site for thirty minutes is more effective than forty-eight hours of actual "work." Who knew?! Well, YOU knew! I certainly didn't as it was not a rational thing to me. How could seeing someone face-to-face for ten minutes matter more than three hours of data entry?! It's magic. Something happens and I still don't know WHAT that is, but it is paramount. I guess it's connection and relationship building. That drop in the bucket with someone means you can ask for something later ONCE instead of twenty times over emails and missed phone calls.

Facetime, part deux: in the office. The same lesson but at home. "But I get MORE done at home!" Well, things happen in the office that just don't happen when you're not there. Connections, creating the DOTS that might connect in that moment of inspiration, or running into someone in the hallway. Teleconferences versus in-person meetings... I mean, logically they SHOULD be the same, but you're missing almost a full DIMENSION of communication. Magic doesn't happen on the phone. I now see that telecommuting should only be out of necessity, not preference. Even now that I'm consulting for MELA, I get A LOT more done when I'm there knocking off TO DO items with the team in the Clin Ops Room (I know that must be a trip to hear!). I can tell you all this now, but when _____ and I started dating, she would get up to teach at 6 am so I would come to work, work out in the gym and then start my day. And I was produc- tive! Don't get me started on the people who just came in early to get coffee for two hours and SAY they got in early (facetime as fake work will NEVER be cool with me)... BUT, by the time lunch came around, I could knock things off BEFORE the meetings started. Instead of cramming to do them after the meetings or at night. Now the work at night was extra. I mean, don't get me wrong, it was still there! But it was more organized.

Leela cared about the company, pure and simple. When it came time to assemble the Pre-Market Approval Application dossier, she really stepped-up, voluntarily. The PMA application is a huge docu- ment that contains virtually all of the data generated over the life of a development project, which spans ten to fifteen years. Orga- nizing, integrating, and designing the flow and overall story is a monumental task. We engaged a medical writer to do, perhaps, the most important part: prepare the five clinical study reports proving that MelaFind did what we said it does for patients. However, the person did not deliver. Leela and Kathy approached me stating that the two of them could write the dossiers and wanted to do so. They volunteered to do more work! I had confidence that they could do it because Leela was an excellent writer and Kathy was great with data. They made a great combination and played off each other very, very effectively. Medical writing is a different animal, but I could help with that because I used to write clinical study reports and dos- siers when I first came into the industry. They did a tremendous job, working closely with our consultant statistician and Principal Sci- entist, Dina. I wrote the integrated summary of the clinical rationale for the product. Their efforts not only were responsible for the PMA being submitted on time; it also provided them the opportunity to master the results and perform more outstanding work one year later in preparing the presentations for the FDA AdComm meeting. The FDA panel voted in favor of the product. This was huge for the company. Without this, we could never have won the fight that then took place to obtain FDA approval one year later.

Now, before this happened, I had difficulty getting Leela to focus and organize herself, take notes, attack her to-do list, understand that her work product is an extension of herself, and attend meetings on time. In the early days of my tenure at the company, I gave a book called *A Sense of Urgency* to everyone in the organization because we needed to transition from a Research focused organization to a Development-centric organization. We needed employees to set deadlines and achieve them, come hell or high water, to see how their contribution affected the contributions of others, which in turn affected the entire project. I impressed this on the organization at every opportunity.

We were also a company with an inordinate number of younger employees; for many of them, this was their first job. They hadn't yet learned the basics of working at an office so we had to show them. The other problem in a small company is that there are no true managers; everyone is working, and classic "management" time basically doesn't exist. Leela, especially, needed to be taught how to work. She was an uncut diamond, but she was as delicate as a flower. So I had to be gentle, but clear, precise, and direct. This was not easy to do. I told her privately that I especially wanted her to read the book and to "become the change" that the company needed. She wasn't ready for it at the time, but as the following reflections from her attest, she certainly did internalize many lessons:

> *Sense of Urgency—remember you bought that book and I didn't read it that weekend and commented that it was ironic that I didn't have a sense of urgency to read the sense of urgency?! Ok, so again in my rational mind, I was like I WILL read it but I got other stuff to do. But when your boss goes out of their way to give you advice and tells you to read a book, you better DO IT because that just became priority! Man, if I were a manager now and that happened, I'd take it as a sign. Thanks for not having taken it as a sign! I was just young and naïve.*

Racing to work—you always said that you should be speed-ing to work. I would always joke that I'm always speeding to work because I'm always late. But the truth is, I was always excited to go to work. Ha! I guess it's unfair of me to judge anyone who didn't feel that way... in fact I think that was a huge flaw I had as a manager... expecting people to "be" like me—specifically, caring as much as I do. I can look over your mistakes if I felt like you cared and wanted to do better!! But the truth is for most people, they just want to correct the mistakes and go home. They don't want or need the mentoring. I've digressed from the original topic into something that perhaps both of us didn't do well (ugh!)—which is expecting others to have the fire that we had. And getting REALLY frustrated or angry when it doesn't happen! Now, that having been said, I do think that (a) people express it differently sometimes and (b) that's fine they just shouldn't be put in a position with more than 1 task (strategist vs. operator?). But it's a good and bad thing. I guess one hopes to impress upon someone like "you," but it probably shouldn't be a per-sonal rebuke when they don't, and don't get it.

Do it as soon as you think about it. So many times we'd be dis-cussing something in a meeting and we'd realize "oh we should ask so and so about whatever"—you'd just pick up the phone and we'd get our answer in five minutes, instead of putting it on a list, prioritiz-ing, and maybe getting to it that day or more likely within the week because inevitable other things would come up. But by having made a move on that one thing, you sort of spring forward instead of build-ing a wall of "I gotta get to that's."

Show up fifteen minutes before work or meetings—I learned this in a funny way. You mentioned it because you said that there was no one at MELA (meaning me!) teaching new recruits lessons like that. If work starts at 9, plan to show up at 8:45. I missed the boat on that one—it's not your fault!

Taking notes—I STILL tell people that the CEO of my com-pany takes notes ALL THE TIME! My friend gets so annoyed when she's training someone and they're not taking notes. It's definitely a sign! You have notebooks filled with your awesome notes. You're ridiculously smart and would've probably remembered all that anyway, but that's what makes you even more unstoppable. I can't imagine ever going into a meeting and NOT taking notes.

Formatting—ok this is a big lesson that I still embody and pass on to others. Boy did I come a long way in this! My documents are gorgeous now! How many CEOs know more about PDF, PowerPoint, and Excel than most of the people who work for them? Yeah, none. PRIDE in the way work is done and presented is another big lesson that I've learned from you and have tried to impart. My biggest pet peeve now is when people don't understand the purpose of Excel— you can't write "Y" and "yes" and "1" to all mean the same thing!!!!! Argh!!! Anyway, I remember when you initiated one of the first pivotal sites back when I just started working at MELA. I packed a box of supplies and it was a mess. You told me it was a mess but you weren't critical you just mentioned it should be presented better. Just a small thing like that was a big deal to me and lord knows the boxes look a lot better now! That having been said, I am NOT applying this rule of perfection to this document because I just want to blurt everything and not obsess because then I'll never get it to you... which leads me to:

Deadlines—remember how bad I was at that? Ok, I still am struggling. Focusing on one project and not fifty has made it a lot better for me but you taught me that not hitting deadlines results in low/bad quality. So here I am thinking that I want to do things to perfection, but I realized that holding a project up has the same if not worse effect than just sending in what you have and going from there.

Leela emerged as a leader in the company. Soon, she was mentoring others. As I saw her develop, I challenged her to assume a stronger role—she liked to observe and perform, rather than be vocal, challenge, and make pronouncements. Managers need to know when which of these two behaviors is warranted. I started getting more forceful with her also because I had built up a reservoir of good will with her—she knew the make-up of my heart and soul, so I could be a little more direct with her. When I told her she needed to step up and speak up, she told me that she didn't like to do that because she did not want to be considered pedantic and arrogant. There is no way that she could ever be considered arrogant, and her reticence to take the leap was stopping her from being the kind of leader the company needed her to be. And I told her that, quite emphatically. As she reflected:

> You're not arrogant, Leela—this is a story I tell a lot. We were in your office and you schooled me! You knew that I was really worried about being seen as arrogant, and you said point blank: there's nothing you can do that will make someone think you're arrogant so stop thinking of it. In fact, it is HOLDING YOU BACK.

Leela is someone I will never forget. I felt privileged to have played such a big part in her life. I also felt responsible for her. Working with her really sums up the fundamental message of the book—selflessly caring is good for business. I cared about the company, the patients, the employees, and the shareholders more than I cared about myself. I found a way to proceed that optimized the outcome for all stakeholders. As you read in her comments above, she also selflessly cared. I think selfless caring begets selfless caring, too. If you want people to behave in a certain way, you need to model that behavior, yourself. I tried to do that, as I mentioned in Chapter 5—as you can see by this insight from Leela, she noticed:

> You were kind of the best at everything—ok, probably not EVERY-THING, but your breadth and depth of skills was ridick. I mean, the high level at which you were operating is unimaginable to me sometimes. Remember how you also protected us from the outside world—we only saw you as a President, but apparently as I've learned CEO has a whole other set of duties that you did under the radar. And just even being a great writer! All these things raise the bar significantly for anyone who works with you. Or at least they should and would really p-ss me off when people didn't notice that and at least TRY to reach for that!

Unfinished Products

I have had the honor, privilege, and pleasure of working with many tremendous people to whom I owe a great deal. I have written fondly about several young people, eager and full of potential, for whom I made special efforts to guide—Alexei, Jenna, Zack, Alex, and Leela. I have also mentioned some great hires who were more advanced in their careers and contributed mightily, and without whom, the projects would not have been successful—Vivian, Claudia, Al, Janice, and Jeff. There were two people that I hired and managed who were somewhere in the middle—advanced in their careers, yet, still having so much more potential. These two were truly unfinished products: having concrete skills to offer that required virtually no refinement or training (hence, "products"), but having so much still untapped in them that their potential exceeded their current reality. I mentioned one already—Denise Webber, who joined me at Anthra from Cytogen, where she was the most underutilized resource in the company. The other is Diana Garcia-Redruello.

How do you manage people like this? You've hired them to fill a void—and they have the skills to do it. But you see so much more in them that compels you to turn them loose in new areas and see what can happen. Of course, they will need training and guidance in the new areas. Many managers do not appreciate the potential in employees like these, rather they focus on the clear and immediate needs for which the employees were hired. That is a shame, and managers who selflessly care about the company and the employees can spot this potential and talent, then foster and nurture it.

Diana was a ballerina at Lincoln Center from the age of six to sixteen. She worked on Wall Street for a couple of years in South American Markets, then she worked at Jurlique and L'Occitane En Provence, consumer dermatology companies. We hired her to run our consumer outreach effort for MelaFind. Since the way to catch melanoma early was for patients to be cognizant of the issue and to undergo regular skin exams; we needed to mobilize patients.

When Diana joined, it was clear to all of us that she had much more skill than that; she had tremendous people skills (able to read body language and satisfy needs), combined with intelligence, insight, and savvy so I also asked her to help out with investor relations and public relations. Then, I asked her to lead the ex-US sales and marketing efforts of MelaFind, which she did, reluctantly, launching the product and running the commercial operations in Germany and Austria.

Here are the reflections that Diana provided for the book:

One-size-does-NOT-fit-all: he took the interest and care to get to know you, your strengths and weaknesses. He then managed you within that personalized frame to help you grow and perform at a level higher than you may have envisioned for yourself (and that was also beneficial to the project and company). Everyone wins!

Employees are human beings, unique and different and wonderful. Employee manuals and policies are good lines in the road, but an effective manager must see the individual and tailor his or her approach, accordingly. Diana continued:

Innovative: he always supported non-conventional business strategies and marketing plans. This enabled me to develop content marketing that was key to mobilizing patients and converting/recruiting customers.

This clearly goes to trial and error and reinvention—especially when you are doing things that have never been done before, being empirical is a must. But even when tackling problems that are not rocket science or new, trial and error with rapid learning and adjustment is critical. Diana added:

Diverse: he promoted diversity not only in professional expertise, but in different cultural backgrounds and genders. This was a key fundamental that helped teams work together on a global level and cross-functionally, as well as share different ideas. He under-stood that women are underrepresented in boardrooms, at senior executive levels, and in business in general. He was very proactive in understanding the needs and actively supported the careers of women while promoting a "more women in the workplace" environ-ment. He never conducted a meeting without female representation.

I embraced diversity when I was at MELA. How could you not when you are exposed to these phenomenal minds from different corners of the earth who are just so incredibly different than you, and success is dependent upon their contributions? This taught me to look for the mutant view even in attacking more mundane matters. Obtaining the perspectives of different people makes for better decision-making and for effective defense of the decisions that are made.

As Alex said in Chapter 3, I am a feminist. Early-on at MELA I instituted a policy that no meeting could be conducted without a woman in the room. It was a serious policy. Several times, when our woman leaders were not around, the engineering team needed to ask our accounts receivable/payable staffer to join the meet-ing; she loved it, even though she didn't understand much. We had very strong women leaders—heads of Clinical, Marketing, Human Resources, as well as Chief Scientist. One of our early CFOs was a woman, as well. Four of my seven direct reports (excluding an administrative assistant) were women. I also put four women on the board, giving us a 50/50 gender split. These actions sent a resound-ing message throughout the company and to our customers. Diana also stated:

Inspires (inspire you to aspire for more, healthy ambition): he helps you push yourself beyond your own limits, helping you capitalize on your strengths while growing past your weaknesses. I person-ally experienced this with the German market launch. On many occasions, I felt I didn't possess the expertise needed to execute a full market launch in a foreign country without the benefit of the language or a full team, but he convinced me of the opposite and helped me perform at a much higher level than I could have ever imagined. He was key in inspiring and supporting me during very difficult times and during very successful times. He broke me out of my comfort zone, allowing me to perform (and deliver) many tasks that were not necessarily strengths of mine.

Diana, Leela, Zack, Al, Alexei, and Nyq, had no idea what they were truly capable of achieving. I could see it more clearly than they could. I encouraged them to attack—it was they who saw their weaknesses, I showed them their strengths and together we dealt with the weaknesses when and if they became a problem. I love what Zack had to say in Chapter 1; his desire to reward me for taking a chance on him drove him more than his desire for personal success on the project. Diana went on:

Fosters (relationships & connections). Promoted team work and helped others achieve for the greater good of the goals set forth. He relished team work and team dinners. This helped me foster relationships with internal stakeholders, as well as with my own team members. We became a small family (of sorts), and we were happy to work hard and support each other for the greater good of the project.

I truly loved breaking bread with the team. So much more can be done over dinner to win over hearts and minds and instill confidence and cultivate comradery than can be done at the office. One of the things that I did all the time was give up my power to whomever needed it. When I asked Claudia to take over as head of Commercialization for MelaFind, she soon had the largest department in the company. At every team event and dinner, I put Claudia at the head of the table and I made her emcee the proceedings. Of course, I would say a few words, but it would be only when Claudia visibly prompted me to do so. She would thank me every time—she grew into her authority with grace and strength, and everyone knew that she had my full support just from these gestures. Diana further provided:

> *Cares about you: He always invested professional and personal time with you. He helped me become more disciplined and accountable, enabling me to better execute the Company vision. He helped many of us become healthy, functional, cohesive leaders.*

In Chapter 3, I said that maybe Alexei should have written the book; well, maybe Diana and Alexei should have done it! Selfless caring is something that inspires employees and creates for them a safe cocoon within which they can flourish. Diana concluded:

> *Educates (teaches you without you even knowing): He was so very abundant with his time and interest in teaching and coaching me. I always felt comfortable asking him a question whether it was a product related one, a corporate one. or even a political one. He somehow managed to teach you something valuable without you even noticing. I benefited from this during the German market launch where I used so many of the things he taught me either directly or by watching him present or speak. He is a great educator, teacher and cultivator of talent. I am living proof.*

To my delight, several people—Jenna, Leela, and Diana—have expressed the same thing, that is, they felt that I taught them without explicitly teaching. As I mentioned in Chapter 3, I purposely set out never to make people feel I was teaching them anything, and it seems to have worked.

How Do You Know?

How do you know which employees you should take chances on and which of them are not capable of the challenge? When it came to Nyq, Dina told me he is all that and more, and Dina is a mental goddess. Further, I observed Nyq's work ethic and listened to what he had to say and saw his work product over the course of a few months. So I was very comfortable ordaining him head of software and algorithms. With respect to inviting him to be Project Team Leader and in charge of the Askion re-engineering and design-for-manufacturing effort, he showed himself to be competent in many of the necessary skills, and also the team at Askion liked and respected him, in particular, Dieter Enders, who was the program manager. So I pushed Nyq to go outside of his comfort zone because he was already an integral piece, and he had a support partner in Dieter. Also, Nyq was honest, to a fault, if that is possible. He would tell me immediately when he was up against something that the he and the resources that he commanded could not lick. So trust was another huge element with Nyq—I trusted him implicitly because he earned it.

Claudia had sales and marketing experience at blue-chip companies including Pfizer, Merck, and Schering, so she was well trained. I observed her for six months and saw that she adapted well to our small company. Often, people from larger companies do not perform well in smaller ones because they are accustomed to having more support and seldom see the whole project because their previous jobs were very specialized. Claudia showed that she rolled-up her sleeves and did more than her job description, and she mastered the product. But, the major reason I asked Claudia to take over as head of commercialization at MELA was because of her style; she exuded a maturity and calm I have never seen in someone her age. Even though she would speak only when having command of her facts, she was no wallflower; she had leadership presence in the way she comported herself. I knew she could do the job, even if she hadn't done it before. And, we provided her with support, someone who had done it before, as a consultant.

Denise had many of the skills needed from her years as a clinical coordinator of clinical studies and in medical affairs. I asked her to take over the clinical and data departments at Anthra because she showed maturity and a dogged determination to do a good job.

She was a highly competitive athlete and hated losing; I knew she would give it her all. Also, I ran these departments previously, so I assured Denise that I could help her when she had a problem, and she trusted me. We also provided her support from a consultant statistical expert to work with her on the data end.

Diana had a tremendous amount of savvy and comfort around people. She could win over any person under any set of circumstances. And, she knew the product very well, having put the time in to learn it, even though she was not there from the beginning. She also had family in Europe, so asking her to head up the sales and marketing efforts in Germany, did not seem like a far stretch. But, she had never done it before and she was still apprehensive, not wanting to do it. I told her that I would spend a week per month with her visiting customers and attending meetings, and that we would do it together, that she would not be alone, and that she would not be blamed if it didn't go well. She believed me.

So for Nyq, Claudia, Diana, and Denise, as well as for the others whom I already discussed (Leela, Al, Zack), the critical elements were:

1. Competence at their current jobs,
2. Two-way trust,
3. Proper support system, and
4. The right attitude.

I will take chances on people all day long if these ingredients are present. You cannot take a major chance on someone you don't know well. But you can take little chances on them in getting to know them and testing their mettle. For example, when Leela wrote the expedited review application; she did a great job in that small matter, so she earned my trust for larger matters.

At the end of the day, you really don't know. And this is where your comfort with trial and error comes into play—assessment and quick correction based on results follows. And, sometimes, the person on whom you take a chance based on relevant related experience is not successful at the job. I have had that happen a few times. But it taught me a lot about who I can challenge; because of those failed experiences, I learned to focus on the two-way trust and attitude more in determining the people on whom I can take a big chance.

Why Take Chances on People?

The benefits of taking a chance on people rather than either doing it yourself or hiring someone who has done it before are varied:

1. **Competition for talent:** especially for small companies, attracting talent is very difficult. Because of the financial position of the start-up, small companies cannot compete with more established companies with respect to salary, benefits, and job security.

2. **Customization:** a person who has not done the job before, by definition, does not have experience. But that is not necessarily a bad thing, and in small entrepreneurial companies it can be a real asset because the person has no pre-conceived notions of how it is "supposed to be done," so she can put in place policies and solutions that are more aligned with the problems and challenges inherent in the immediate situation, rather than the circumstances for which structures and policies used in prior lives were put in place.

3. **Creativity:** taking a chance on someone allows for out-of-the-box thinking and creativity to be infused into the job at hand. With a clean slate and no failed experience coloring their view, novices are more apt to try a wider range of strategies, thereby having a higher likelihood of implementing creative solutions than a person with significant experience.

4. **Loyalty:** when someone on whom you have taken a chance is successful, he or she feels a tremendous devotion and dedication to the company and the people who gave them the opportunity to flourish. They attack their jobs, initially trying to prove they deserve the chance and not wanting to let down the manager who made it happen, and then later because of pride on a job well-done, which is truly their work.

Taking chances on people and cultivating the talent that they have shown in other areas in order for them to flourish in new and larger arenas makes great business sense. It is also personally rewarding for the manager and leader. I mentioned in Chapter 1 that Zack is taking an executive business training course at Harvard Business School; he says that he would never have been accepted if not for the opportunity that I gave him. I couldn't be more proud. He and the others have expressed their desire to work with me again; I should be so lucky.

Sobering Realities

Although I hate to admit this, not all employees have the make-up or desire to become outstanding performers. That's why it is not always possible to take chances on people whom you know have the talent. They need to demonstrate to you that they have the interest as well as the drive and dedication.

I always believed that if people worked harder and made their jobs their first, second, and third priority, they could accomplish truly great things. And I set out to inspire them to do so, to fall in love with their jobs and careers, as I had done. When they did not respond, it was a source of great disappointment and anguish for me. Vivian and Julie disabused me of this. True, they told me every employee who works harder and longer and makes their job their top priority will perform better. However, those behaviors will not transform them to MVP status.

Tazewell Wilson, a tremendously talented and insightful virologist trained at Rockefeller Institute and who worked with me at Anthra Pharmaceuticals, once said to me, "I love you Joseph, because you believe in the eternal betterment of man." And I do. But, Vivian and Julie taught me that not all people have the core ability or attitude to achieve to the heavens. And I should not get upset or disappointed about that, rather I needed to manage them from where they are.

I begrudgingly accepted the lesson and realized that the "B" players are actually critical and a company cannot function without them. I also learned that they need to be taught and mentored and cared for, and I had to find a way (trial and error) to resonate with them, motivate them, and make them fulfilled in their jobs. Putting them in appropriate circumstances and managing them such that their work was of A quality is the goal, and often, it can be achieved. Selfless caring is not limited to the people with whom a manager and leader most relates. No, it is for everyone whom a manager has the privilege of influencing. So I adjusted my thinking, my expectations, and my approach.

Leela had a big problem with this issue, as well, and I helped her understand the value of "B" players and how to get A quality from them:

> There needs to be more B's than A's. Everyone wants to think they're an A. But you need the B's! A's are innovative, quick and emotional and get stuff done. But you need worker bees who are great at that one or two things (not an insult, the A's clearly can't do THOSE things) to make it all happen—to execute the vision without questioning every part of it. I don't think anything would ever get done if you had more A's than B's. I mean, even in a band situation, I've actually fired people who are more on the "Artist" spectrum than the "get it done" spectrum... I think the same is definitely true about a

company like MELA's, and any endeavor that is inherently creative and innovative. There is a vision held by one person, or a small group of people... everyone else's job is to make that vision happen, not critique the vision. If that were the case, nothing would happen (too many cooks in the kitchen analogy perhaps).

Sometimes, Someone Who Believes in You is All You Need

I learned to take chances on people when someone took a chance on me. When I was in eighth grade, I was selected as the player to represent our town on the county All-Star basketball team. I was a big fish in a very small town, but Bergen County had some big towns in it with lots of really good players. When I arrived in Hasbrouck Heights for the first night of tryouts, I was very nervous. I knew no one and I was amidst the best players in the county who were trying to outdo each other. I am a pass-first player—I always preferred to set up others for the shot than to take it myself. I was very team focused. This was not a time to be team focused, as I observed because the guys were playing hard and trying to make the players around them look bad so that they would be selected.

I made each cut on the subsequent nights of tryouts and practice. On the third night, the coach, a man I had never met in my life, came up to me and told me that I would be the starting point guard. Wow, the point guard is the general of the team. He calls out the plays on offense, brings the ball up, creates opportunities for others, and also puts the defense in the right position. But, I was frightened and intimidated, so I thanked the coach and then told him that Billy is a better player than I am. The coach smiled and put his hand on my shoulder and said, "You actually are right, Billy is a better player. But, you can dribble the ball with both hands without looking at it, and you listen." I knew that I did both of the things that the coach said, so I said okay. And we practiced with me as the starting point guard.

When the game came, all of us were very nervous. I played for the whole first quarter, half of the second quarter, the back half of the third quarter, and the entire fourth quarter. It was a see-saw game: I did what I was supposed to do, what the coach told me to do when he told me to do it—dishing out assists, bringing up the ball, and making sure everyone was in place given the play that I called and defensive we were running. With a minute and a half left in the game, I made a play on a long pass the other team made against our zone and I got fouled. Free throws were not my strong suit—I was about a sixty percent free throw shooter. We were down by one point, sixty-three to sixty-two, and I went to the foul line for a one-and-one, which means if you miss the first you don't get a second. I hit both. On the next inbounds throw from the other team, I intercepted the ball and quickly evaded a defender who wanted to foul me to stop the clock, dribbled around a little to take some time off the clock and draw a double team, then passed the ball to our wide open forward who made the layup. Now we were up by three. I was then part of a trap on the next inbounds pass that caused the other team to waste lots of time, and they took an errant shot, missing it. We took possession and won.

While I was still on the court, a father of one of my teammates, a man I had also never met before that moment, rushed up to me and told me that he had never seen a player at my age have such court savvy. He said that I seemed to always be in the right place at the right time. I thanked him and then asked my coach, who was in the stands, what court savvy meant. He said it means situational awareness.

This experience is still indelibly etched in my mind not for the on-court performance—I have had better stats before and after that game—but for the coach. He saw something in me that I did not see in myself. I was frightened and he gave me confidence. He did not lie; he told me what I did well and how he was going to leverage those strengths. He taught me that being successful is to have some requisite level of skill (dribbling with both hands without looking at it) and having the right attitude (listening). And so I have passed this on, and taken chances on as many employees that I have had the privilege of managing who have some talent and the right attitude. And, it works.

CHAPTER 7

Management & Leadership Tips & Insights

In the previous chapters, I have explained that selfless caring is necessary in two key activities in order for a manager and leader to be successful:

1. Relentlessly complete preparation
2. Dogged trial and error and reinvention

We have provided real-life examples of both of these behaviors leading ultimately to right and winning solution. We have also discussed how selfless caring, manifest in these two behaviors, inspires and energizes the work force, peers, partners, and other stakeholders. Selflessly caring also enables true personal leadership, alignment, and "followership."

Yes, selfless caring is the bedrock principle that has been responsible for the successes I have enjoyed as well as the insights I have developed over more than two decades of managing. It has been the foundational principle that has inspired and pushed me to make my best decisions, produce my best work, and develop my most effective leadership and management strategies and techniques.

What follows are some of the lessons and strategies I have learned and developed by selflessly caring. (Some of these principles have been featured in *Fast Company, Inc.com, SmartBriefs, Smart-Blogs,* and *Venture Beat.*)

Do You Want to Be a Boss or a Leader?

I was having a cup of coffee with a former work colleague who lamented over what happened at a meeting with his employer when the CEO said many things that were, shall we say, less than inspiring. The episode really called into question the CEO's leadership ability in the eyes of my friend and his colleagues.

I stressed to my friend that, if he wanted to thrive there, he needed to look past this one event and try to find something about the CEO that inspires him and gives him confidence because you cannot work for someone for whom you have no respect. Consider this the worst that this individual can be, and remember that you got through it, and move on.

Contradicting myself, I then laughed and quoted the movie *Starman,* in which Jeff Bridges' character tells a government alien-life investigator why his kind are interested in our kind: "Humans are a strange species... you are at your very best when things are at their worst."

My friend quickly said, "Not all humans."

That is very true. Not all humans, indeed. But leaders are not "all humans." More is expected of them.

Great leaders are at their best when things are at their worst. Anyone can be considered a good leader when things are humming along without a hitch. It is easy to align employees and maintain a great vibe in a company when profits are soaring, or you recently moved into really cool new space and bonus checks were distributed.

Try leading when a new competitor has taken away significant market share, when your manufacturing partner's facility is
destroyed by fire, or when the FDA delays your new drug approval
indefinitely after you have hired and trained a new sales force. Try
leading when Wall Street analysts downgrade your stock, when a
licensing deal that you were working on for a year falls through, or
when the patent for your main product has expired. These are the
times when a boss earns the title of "leader" because these are the
times when employees are looking for leadership. They are wonder-
ing, "What are we going to do?"; "Will everything be all right?"; "Can
we make it through this? "and "I'm frightened." If the boss does not
have something to say and a plan to address these fears, he or she will
never be considered a leader.

Returning to the *Starman* theme, I offer five lessons to managers who want to be great leaders:

1. Be your best when conditions are at their worst.
2. Make maps; that is the job that the alien who cloned Scott
   Hayden's body tells a stranger that he does for a living.
   Leaders make the maps because they know where they
   want to go, and they have the skill to chart the course.
   Leaders also don't look in the rear-view mirror.
3. Exercise focused power for critical path items. The alien
   had a handful of silver beads with unlimited power; however, he used them for very specific purposes to achieve his
   objective with minimal to no collateral damage.
4. Use some power to save a wounded deer. Build up the weak
   and teach them to do better, rather than pushing them
   down to make your own standing greater.
5. Go very fast at yellow lights. Leaders step up to the front,
   quickly, at the first sign of a threat to the business.

Just like Jenny Hayden, who watched in awe and helped Starman as he did all of these things and more, your employees are

constantly watching you, and even more so when the chips are down. Put on a good show at the most critical and even dire moments, and they might help you, and then even consider you a leader.

Most importantly, do not negate years of good performance—dare I say leadership—with one stupid word or action that you did not think through fully. Just like moviegoers, employees will turn on the hero when he does not act heroically. The reservoir of good will is a lot shallower than you think.

If you want to be great leader, be a hero.

Ten Tips for Leading through Changes

To transition your business to a more innovative company, you will need to guide a highly trained and skilled work force through some difficult changes.

As the boss, you may not have the same IQ as the smartest guys in the office, but it is your job to lead and align these high achievers, which often involves disrupting the status quo.

Ensuring that your team of geniuses is aligned with the goal, providing actionable insights, and interacting with other members of the team are critical to success.

Here are ten items managers need to consider when leading their teams through change:

1. **IMMEDIATE RESULTS ARE NOT POSSIBLE:** Anticipate that creating an alternate alignment will take six to twelve months, especially if you are new to the team. Be flexible and patient and realize that you are working on a mosaic masterpiece and there is no way of knowing exactly what it will look like on day one. Be confident that it will be beautiful in the end, no matter what, and share that confidence.

2. **CHANGE CAUSES FEAR, AND FEAR STIFLES:** You are not here to change your employees; you are here to change the trajectory of the business or project. Make them comfortable, not off balance. Geniuses are not mind readers; they will read your actions for signs of things to fear. Don't give them easy things—like changing everything—to be upset about!

3. **ORDAIN EACH EMPLOYEE A LEADER OF SOMETHING:** Many high achievers want to be recognized for their achievements. And in the end, it's about getting some work done, even if it isn't fully integrated and coordinated.

4. **INVITE THEM INTO CRAFTING THE PROBLEM STATEMENT:** Don't do it on your own or you'll be seen as objecting to the employees' way of getting things done. Once your high achievers can see that things are not optimal on their own, you will have created a window for change to actually occur.

5. **DO IT THEIR WAY, FOR A WHILE:** Invite staff to craft a solution and use their input; don't simply take it under advisement. Show them that you can learn from them. You will benefit and become a better manager for it.

6. **AVOID POSITIONAL AUTHORITY:** Avoid the temptation to assert positional authority when you get exasperated. There will likely be some movement and then retrenchment back to the same or even worse behaviors. You will make mistakes, too. Having a positive and optimistic attitude and cheerleading is your job. Telling your team to do something "because you said so" doesn't work.

7. **EXERT PERSONAL AUTHORITY BY LETTING YOUR TALENT SHOW:** Deliver on a few major projects that really matter, and a couple that don't. Once your

employees see you do something that they could not do themselves, or that they have tried to do and failed (like getting more money for the project), they will begin to see the value that you bring and respect you.

8. **DEFINE YOUR TEAM:** You will quickly learn which of these people the super-geniuses are, which of them are followed by their peers, and which ones are beginning to warm to your lead. These individuals will have a few disciples within the organization who will have figured out what you just figured out. Poof, you just identified the change masters.

9. **GO SLOW AND STEADY:** With the blessing and cooperation of your change masters, start doing what needs to be done to make the operation all that it can be. Go slowly, but steadily, and maintain the alignment of the core group as you go.

10. **DETERMINE WHO IS ON THE BUS AND WHO IS OFF THE BUS—THEN CLOSE THE DOOR AND DRIVE:** At some point, the others will come in line, and there will be no dramatic showdown. Disruption, if needed, for the good of the project and the company will be tolerated at this point by the ones who matter most.

Ten Strategies for Attracting and Maintaining a Top-Notch Team

Barring very few exceptions, startups are cash poor and remain so for a very long time. But driven founders are capable of thriving in this environment and are not dissuaded by uncertainty of outcome or income. Compensation is rarely the motive in their pursuit of success.

New employees with additional technical, regulatory, and business competencies are required as the startup progresses. The newcomers to the team typically have a different skill set than entrepreneurs and, unlike founders, they may require real salaries.

The dilemma is how to attract and retain talent in startups, which by their nature, are highly uncertain and cash-strapped enterprises.

Here are ten important tips that worked for me:

1. **Be passionate and share the vision.** The goal of what can be achieved must be big enough to employees, i.e., the public good, affecting lives, big monetary payout, and unique or rich experiences that further their careers. Explain the reason why you are so inspired by the enterprise. Companies with less than three years of cash will likely attract younger employees and those willing to roll the dice, thereby pre-selecting for a group of employees for whom passion, vision, and other forms of compensation resonate.

2. **Ask candidates and current employees what they want.** Ask what they are trying to obtain through their jobs. I always ask that question on interviews. I also tell candidates that if I can't deliver on what they seek within the first three to six months, I will not offer them the job.

3. **Give them something that their friends in other companies are not getting—responsibility, mentorship, exposure, fun, excitement, and a community feeling.** Give them something that their parents never got on the job—respect, appreciation, inclusion, and a feeling of importance. Employees, especially younger ones, talk to their friends and family often. By having their network tell them that they are getting more by being with you, they will continue to take a chance with a company that is not flush with cash.

4. **Over-communicate.** Not knowing is frightening; knowing is empowering, even if it is not pleasant. Give them important information about the entire business operation. This will lead them to feel vested in the company, not simply their own jobs.

5. **Say THANK YOU, often.** When an employee is thanked for a contribution, even if it is part of the job description, the person feels appreciated, and feels like a peer not a subject.

6. **Know everyone's name and what each person does.** Walk the floors and point out to each employee how his or her job is critical to the success of the company. This shows your appreciation of the work they are doing.

7. **Work WITH, not FOR.** NEVER introduce or refer to an employee as someone who works FOR you; rather say this person or that person works WITH you. Believe me, their friends at other companies are not receiving the personal attention of points 5, 6, and 7, and chances are their parents have not in their entire careers.

8. **Have regular company meetings where you're not the one doing all the talking.** Let the managers present details about what is going on in their department. Recognize monthly individual performers who embody a company value, or who perform at a very high level, and give them a small award. Creating a community environment is crucial when resources are scarce.

9. **Own the fact that you need to lead.** You cannot trust that your managers are modeling your behavior; rather you need to touch the lives of every employee regularly. Rotating morning breakfasts with each department is a good way to make sure that employees continue to see and hear the message and invest in the leader.

10. **Stress the benefits, regardless of outcome.** Make staffers understand that if things ultimately don't work out for the company or project, they will still have benefitted for the experience and be able to build on it. Explain to all employees what they have learned and how they can leverage it in the future. Reminding employees of the skills they're receiving, apart from a paycheck, gives them reasons to continue to believe and invest themselves in the company and to tolerate the uncertainty that comes with working at a startup.

Six Tips on What to Do When It Hits the Fan

If you do anything long enough, you will inevitably confront seemingly insurmountable hurdles that may or may not be possible to clear. That's not a crisis. I learned the hard way what a true crisis is: a shocking, unpredictable, and catastrophic event foisted upon your company that threatens its immediate survival and rocks all of its stakeholders to the core. Startups are more likely to face true crises than established businesses. So how are you going to lead your company through your crisis? This is how I got through mine successfully:

1. **Own it.** Shock and denial were my first reactions when the FDA issued what turned out to be an unlawful "rejection" letter even though we did everything the way it told us to, and even when the clinical trial data met all pre-specified endpoints. I wanted to believe that it was just a bad dream. I remember telling myself that I was grieving and didn't have time for all five stages of the grief cycle, so stop denying it; don't look for scapegoats; don't make excuses; don't offer reasons. I owned the fact that the crisis had arrived— that's all that matters. And it was my crisis, and I made it

the only ten things on my ten-point to-do list. I told myself that this is why you were given the title, and now it's time to earn your keep. Somehow, some way, you are going to find a way to win.

2. **Assemble the team.** Even though the crisis was mine, I needed help from different quarters. We created a team of the best and brightest and most creative, inside and outside the company, from the major disciplines that were needed to manage the disaster. Some members suggested we needed help in areas I hadn't considered and so we set out to get experts from those disciplines. We had regular group meetings at least once per week, in addition to meetings with individuals on the team who were in charge of specific areas of managing the crisis. I chaired the meetings myself. Although this was my crisis, and I was the leader, I knew that I could not solve it alone.

3. **Embrace the uncertainty.** We were in unchartered territory. Without realizing it, we exercised the Scientific Method until we found something that worked—Francis Bacon would have been proud. Trial and error within the multi-component, parallel set of strategies and tactics was required, and so we tried and failed, a lot. One of the hardest things was to give a plan enough time to start to show signs of working, while not wasting time before nixing things that didn't work. It was also difficult to maintain alternatives for as long as possible, not irrevocably committing to a strategy that might not work to the exclusion of other alternatives. The opinion of the multi-disciplinary team of experts helped, but in the end, that decision was on me, and will be on you.

4. **Commit to a single-minded focus and delegate.** Many employees and consultants would approach me and ask

how they could help. But, dealing with the crisis was the domain of a small group. I realized that I had to have a tireless and single minded focus and that anything not in service of solving the crisis was a distraction and superfluous. Because of the passion of so many other managers and employees, I was able to delegate everything else. Managing the crisis was the most important thing that I could be doing, and it often required getting ideas from other members of the team, which is very difficult and all-consuming. I appointed others within the business, people not on the crisis team, to manage all other priorities of the company. This was a tremendous blessing as more employees and managers realized that they were important to the company and made great contributions.

5. **Prepare, reinvent, and be schizophrenic.** I had to be an engine of activity and the driving force. The process required that I immerse myself into every aspect of the strategies and tactics because I was the central repository of all information about the multi-disciplinary plan and tactics. Moreover, I had to accept the fact that I was at the helm when the problem happened; therefore, the way I was going about things got us into this mess, so it was unlikely that the same sort of thinking/approach would get us out of it. I had to force myself to consider drastically different approaches and ways of thinking by being schizophrenic (metaphorically). Coming at the problem from all sides that I could think of allowed me to accept good ideas from anywhere.

6. **Be Jerry West.** I remembered what my basketball camp coach told me about the basketball player Jerry West (the NBA logo). What made him great was that in the huddles at crunch times with ten seconds left when the coach would

ask the team, "Who wants the ball?" Jerry West said, "I want the ball." So I had to want the ball, and to take the last shot. You'll have to take the last shot; take it and when it swishes, declare it a TEAM win.

Five Tips for Connecting with Your Audience

As the leader of a business, especially a startup, your job is to connect with audiences ranging from potential or current investors, employees, corporate partners, customers, regulatory bodies, or boards. This is a skill that many first-time CEOs need to develop. Even if you are gregarious by nature, or in my case, was a lector at Sunday Mass since I was ten-years-old, understanding how best to connect with an audience in business is critical for your success. Here are five strategies that I learned over the years:

1. **Truly want to connect with your audience.** I was once asked by the CEO "How do you do it; how do you keep it fresh?" We were raising money, telling the story to investor after investor and he noticed that my energy and enthusiasm never faded and that I told the story a different way every time. The key for me is that I genuinely wanted to connect with the audience. I enjoyed telling the story and I defined myself by whether the target received the message and stayed engaged. A mentor of mine once said that it is more about what is going on in their shop than your shop. Nonsense—that's for rationalization later when I fail; in the moment, my whole being and self-worth is wrapped up in connecting with my audience.

2. **Research your audience and engage them, early and often.** I learned from a CEO who knew more about the companies we were visiting than the people running them. When I am greeted at the elevator by the people with

whom I am meeting, I don't talk about how Google Maps sent me four blocks away. Instead, I aim to get as much information from them as I can before the presentation starts. I want to learn things about the people and their most recent experiences so that I can best use that material to make my message relevant. For investors, I often find out whether they were in the last deal of a company with a similar platform or product that just made the news. Then, I know how to play slide six of my presentation. I often ask them about their experiences with specific issues that I am discussing or about to discuss. They appreciate my eagerness to learn from them, and it gives them an opportunity to talk. It's all business, all the time. Knowledge is power, so I do as much reconnaissance before the meeting and get as much intelligence during the meeting as I can.

3. **Dress the part and mind your manners.** I don't let anything get in the way of my message. This often means playing the appropriate role at the appropriate time. When I go to the FDA, I wear beige pants, matte loafers, blue blazer, button-down washed-out blue shirt, muted tie, and everyday watch. For investors, power blue suit, new tie, cool socks, and shiny shoes. For employee meetings, rolled-up sleeves and open top button and casual on Fridays. I never wear cologne. Seriously, the non-verbal communication can squelch the best slides and presentation; don't let it.

4. **View and adapt, and don't go alone.** When I enter a room, I clone myself and place invisible me on a perch where I can see physical me and my audience. I constantly search for signs of engagement and interest and either keep going with the plan and cadence if all is well, or adapt quickly if I am losing my audience. On an IPO roadshow there were two individuals in different meetings who were

not buying what I was selling—the harder I tried, the more I adapted, the less engaged they were. Invisible me noticed that they literally turned their chairs away from me and to one of the scientific founders. What did I do? I made a mental note to understand how I screwed up later, but at the moment, I motioned to the founder to complete the entire presentation, even my slides.

5. **Decide on three things that you want to communicate.** For me, this is not about the data I am presenting or the marketing or development plans, or the use of proceeds, per se. This is about the very few over-arching messages that I want all of the facts I am delivering to serve. For example, we know the market, we are intense, and we have made tremendous progress since the last meeting. I once told the scientific founder who liked to employ the Socratic Method with venture capitalists the three messages that we are going to communicate in the meeting. None of the statements were on any of his slides or mine. I also told him that we are not going to lead them to the water and hope that they drink; instead, we are going to bottle-feed these three messages to them. At the end of the meeting, one of the venture capitalists summarized the session with the exact three over-arching messages that we set out to communicate. I'll never forget the look on the face of my partner.

Five Things that Clueless Bosses Say that Zap Motivation

An aligned and inspired work force is the dream of every true leader. It takes great empathy to connect with employees; in order to lead them, you first need to understand them. How do you truly understand employees? The answer comes from one of the best movie lines in history, delivered by Atticus Finch to his son Gem in *To Kill a Mockingbird*, "You never really understand a person until you consider things from his point of view... Until you climb into his skin and walk around in it."

Employees rarely think about your point of view, but you must understand their point of view. They care about making enough money to buy their daughter a prom dress and their sons new sneakers. They worry about their family's health and childcare. They want to move up in the organization and enhance their earning power. They want to feel empowered and recognized, and they want to be thanked. Their baseline view is that the person in the corner office— please don't tell me that you actually have a corner office (make it a conference room for all to use and move your office, but I digress)— is out of touch with the workers, earns too much, doesn't work as hard as they do, and takes all the credit.

So you've been Myers Brigged, 360'd, coached, and schooled in the six Primal Leadership styles. But, still you don't have the aligned, passionate, and inspired work force that you need. If you ever say one of the following glib, off-the-cuff comments, you will devalue your employees and a devalued employee is not inspired or aligned.

1. **"That's above your pay grade."** I bet you have said this soon after saying that employees are not approaching their work "as if they own the company" or never "think outside the box." Hello, President Cognitive Dissonance, you just delivered a mixed message, and guess which one they are going to internalize? Telling employees that there are pecking orders, codes of conduct, and duties and responsibilities by cast, is simply the stupidest thing a manager can say. You want employees to be unfettered and think of things you haven't. That doesn't happen when they are told to stay in their boxes.

2. **"That's confidential," and its twin brother, "that's on a need-to-know basis and you don't need to know."** In a startup there are very few things that are truly confidential. Startups are flat organizations and information sharing is a huge part of maintaining that culture. Telling employees that something is confidential indicates that you don't trust them, they are not part of the "inner circle," and they are not your peers. Startups are all about a group of peers achieving something amazing. I prefer to trust first—to give people the freedom to show me that they are not trustworthy rather than to assume it. A trust-first culture is truly inspiring.

3. **"Please leave the room while we continue with other matters."** You've invited several managers and employees to a board (or management committee) meeting. The presentations are over and you have other items to discuss with the directors or management committee. What do you say? Don't dismiss them the way a five-star general would do to corporals or privates because they will feel like infantry and await instruction on everything else, rather than taking chances and filling voids that you don't see. There are much savvier ways to have them leave the meeting such as taking a bathroom break.

4. **"My people, my team."** This is occasionally succeeded by, "would follow me through fire." Say the first thing if you want employees to feel like chattel; come with the second statement if you want them to feel like stupid chattel. These statements don't elevate team members; instead they serve to remind them that even on the "team" that is working elbow-to-elbow, there is a hierarchy. It is arrogant and self-serving. It also brings back memories of lunch time in grammar school when kick ball teams were being

selected. But this isn't grammar school; it's business and everyone should behave as if they're in charge. After years of leading effectively, being empathetic and inspirational, you might get employees to follow you over warm coals, but don't say that you see them as lemmings.

5. **"Employees are like my children."** The reason children must leave home is so their parents see them as adults. So telling people from age twenty-five to fifty-five that you think of them as your children conjures up their memories of being dependent and powerless. I always felt that managing was a God-given privilege and a moral responsibility, for sure, just like parenting. Early in my career at a company meeting, the CEO made the analogy; I remember thinking that I met his kids, who ranged from eight to fifteen-years-old, and if that's what he thought of me, I better get a new job! You should nurture employees, but show them they're your peers. And don't say the company is like a family. If you're a really good leader, the employees will say it. And when you hear that, smile to yourself.

Five Hiring Mistakes Rookie Managers Make

Twenty-five years ago, I attended a dinner party for the department leaders of a top international conglomerate when the host made a joke about Human Resources stating that HR means "Helps Rarely." Everyone laughed and nodded; so did I. For years before I ventured into startups, I saw HR simply as a place that employees would go to obtain benefits forms and to complain to no avail. HR would also run events in which few wanted to partake. Worst of all, no one in HR had a clue about the business in which the company engaged, especially research and development, so how could they provide anything, except the party line from the CEO? Yes, HR not only helped rarely, it was useless..., so I thought.

And then I started running startups.

I was the second employee in my first startup as well as the head of the office, and the CEO worked remotely. I hired everyone and I engaged every employee multiple times per day. I hired young people in their first jobs, and in their first management jobs. I was able to communicate my values and approach fairly easily. When I would travel, the employees trusted that when I got back, problems would be solved, and the world would be righted.

Then, we hired the thirteenth employee.

I could not keep up. Sharing my insights and giving a piece of myself to the employees no longer worked as the culture-setting and office dynamic cure-all. We needed someone whose job it was to help manage employees. In a startup, there are no pure managers—bosses and department heads are über-doers. So the task of managing is easily overlooked. And, even when you want to be a good and empathetic manager, at a certain critical mass, you cannot do it alone.

The lesson I learned was not only to get a good HR person before the critical mass threshold for chaos hits in a startup, but also get an HR person who shares your values, is a good teacher, and understands your business and technical challenges. Here are the five mistakes that I made, which the right HR person helped to fix:

1. **I wasn't managing effectively.** My only three qualifications as a manager up to that point were having been badly managed in the past, receiving an MBA, and wanting to be a good manager. Being available to all, trying to solve everyone's problems, being disappointed when employees didn't do what I wanted, and getting angry when employees didn't share my passion or fill obvious voids is not managing. An HR person willing to take me on taught me how to manage—how to communicate clearly, set objectives, provide feedback, listen, redirect, and how to provide specific examples of behavior that is valued and behaviors

that don't hit the mark during performance reviews. That prescription, combined with a desire to nurture and have a positive impact on the lives of the employees, was extremely effective.

2. **The managers of the company were not managing effectively.** Our HR head worked with all the managers and taught them how to: run a department meeting, run a project meeting, dole-out tasks, audit performance, provide positive and negative reinforcement, and when to be tough and when to show compassion. She also worked with every manager in devising the performance review system so that it was appropriate for our business and technical jobs. They owned, refined it, and actually used it, which is an achievement unto itself.

3. **I was not in the office enough to reinforce the values and role-model the behaviors that I wanted.** Having someone whose job it was to make sure that my values and messages were consistently being delivered was crucial. The organization felt less of a void when I wasn't physically present or when I was distracted with other pressing matters. Also I realized that the way I communicated did not always resonate, so having another person of authority communicate her way gave us more reach and coverage.

4. **I didn't realize what it takes to establish a gentle culture, compared to a gotcha culture.** The only way to lead with a soft hand is to have that hand constantly felt guiding and providing positive feedback and taking advantage of the few opportunities that present themselves to drive home a message to employees in a non-threatening and non-punitive manner. Having the HR head, who was a respected manager in her own right, doing this with me, provided that omnipresent positive force.

5. **I was encouraging a culture of dependence.** Again, unafraid to take me head-on, our HR head explained to me how my style of management encouraged employees to readily approach me in order to solve their problems. She told me that this was not good for the organization—since I was not getting my work done, and employees were not developing certain skills, like conflict resolution or creative problem solving. She made me become a little more aloof, and when I did engage with employees in this capacity, to have them offer solutions and then direct them to go try. This worked very well.

In short, I needed a solid HR professional to teach me what I was doing wrong, and help fix the mistakes.

My grandfather once taught me that "the fish stinks from the head." I needed someone to tell me when I stank and to teach me how to deodorize.

The Five Most Important P-words for Success

Twenty years ago, my wife and I were asked to give a talk on the critical success factors in business. I have always been involved with biotech and medtech startups, and my wife has worked for huge scientific and pharmaceutical companies. We thought that this dichotomy would interest the audience, especially if we came up with a list that was applicable to both startups and mature companies.

Starting with the 4 P's of marketing as our model--you know, Product, Price, Place, and Promotion--we debated which P's were most important for business success, and chose these:

1. **Passion.** The ability to find ways to make it happen come what may, to lead with personal authority, to reinvent yourself, and to communicate a purpose all come from a burning passion for what you are doing. The desire to

always do your best is rooted in passion. Pete Rose, who treated every pitch and play, no matter the situation, as if there were two outs in the bottom of the ninth in a tied Game 7 of the World Series, is the epitome of passion. I showed the clip from *Scrooged* in which Bill Murray yells at the head of marketing after being told that a new TV commercial was successful because market research showed that "people want to watch the show." "His passionate response was, "That isn't good enough; they have to be so cared to miss it, so terrified!" That's passion, and it will take you far."

2. **Pragmatism.** You can have all of the energy in the world, and embrace the "us-versus-them" mentality, and break down any wall in your way, but without being pragmatic in your approach, you will get nowhere. Even worse, you will waste a lot of time, money, and organizational energy. The tools of pragmatism are planning and auditing—the ability to set goals and test whether the experiment is working. Pragmatism melts ego; a pragmatic person is not vested in a particular view but rather in what is best for the project and charting the right course for the current terrain. My wife quoted fashion designer Donna Karan, who said of herself, "I have a passion for pragmatism."

3. **Perspective.** Getting past an egocentric view of the world, your business, and your problem is crucial to success. Perspective is what MBA students learn; business schools teach you to think about the entire major outside risk factors that have an impact on your business. Knowing where you are relative to the market and your competitors, as well as the trends and the latest developments in technology and science, comes with an ability to view your work from a distance. Effectively managing people and seeing

the wisdom of the alternative view come with an ability to change your perspective. I showed the clip of Robin Williams in *The Dead Poet's Society* in which he stands on the desk to demonstrate how a change in perspective changes one's perception of reality.

4. **Personality.** Unless your business is literally a "one-man band," or you are truly irreplaceable, being successful in business means being able to work with many different people including employees, investors, customers, regulators, board members, and other stakeholders. Simply put, people want to work with those whom they like and with whom they identify. My wife cited many examples of extremely successful people who were not the brightest bulbs in the chandelier, but who did very well, were protected in layoffs, and always landed great positions because "everyone liked them." She mentioned how often during reviews of employees, managers would make a favorable comment such as "He's a great guy," and gloss over the individual's performance issues. Right or wrong, being liked goes a very, very long way.

When we finished, we asked our audience of more than 200 people to vote on which of the four P's they thought my wife and I would say is the most important one—the preeminent P, so to speak. Virtually everyone's hand was raised when we put Passion to the vote. I laughed and told them that they were simply voting for Bill Murray. We said that in our experience, it is without a doubt, Personality.

Fast forward twenty years and four startups later, what would I say? Well, another P has come into the mix:

5. **Perseverance.** After defeating the FDA in a very public, drawn out, and tragic battle that took everything I had and more, I received an email entitled "Perseverance" from

our lead investor. He was passing along his father's favorite quote and congratulated me for enduring, come what may.

Nothing in the world can take the place of persistence. Talent will not; nothing is more common than unsuccessful men with talent. Genius will not; unrewarded genius is almost a proverb. Education will not; the world is full of educated derelicts. Persistence and determination alone are omnipotent. —Calvin Coolidge

Yes, perseverance got me through that unprecedented battle, and we would not have been successful without it, for sure.

If I could go back in time and knew then what I know now, what would I tell the audience is the most important P?

I would have told them exactly what I said twenty years ago— "Personality, and if you don't have one, go out and get one."

Ten Tips for Joining a Start-Up

It is the norm for universities to offer formal programs in entrepreneurship. But not all students have a desire to start a company from scratch, so what gives? The goal is not only to churn out graduates who will start their own companies, but also to get students ready to work in entrepreneurial companies.

What does that mean? Don't all companies need employees who can calculate a net present value, and who know the 4 P's of marketing? Don't companies need engineers who know CAD and chemists who can analyze an HPLC? Yes, they do, but prospective hires have to be ready to answer ten questions in order to not only get a job in an entrepreneurial company, but also to thrive:

1. **Experience on a team:** Students who genuinely enjoy working with others and who have participated meaningfully in an initiative that required close interaction with others are ideal for startups. Be sure to mention in the

interview the national meeting your team organized, or the e-newspaper you started, or the problem that you and your team solved at the school, as well as how you were energized by the social engagement of being on a team.

2. **Passion and motivation:** Fully absorbed and energized from the experience—demonstrating passion for something and having attained what psychologists call the flow state or zone in some project is critical. Your potential employer will be looking to understand the reasons that the experience energized and motivated you and the personal value that you derived from it. If the project at the startup offers something close to that personal value, you're a lock for the job!

3. **Marathon experience:** Many people, especially young people, can be energized for a short period of time (sprinters) or for projects that interest them. The sign of a person ready to contribute seriously to a fledgling company is demonstrating reliability and discipline by being available with the same level of energy for any challenge, big or small, at any time. Employees who can hit the 19th item on the list with the same vigor as the first is what a startup is looking for because, Lord knows, the hours are not nine to five.

4. **Being simply the best:** HBO used to promote this as its catch phrase. I loved those commercials and employers love hires who give their best effort all the time to every project. Never convey that a job or a project is a stepping stone to something else; stress the project before you is critical and you will give it all you have. Giving examples of this kind of work ethic will serve you well, especially if they involve jobs you have held in school, or better yet, internships.

5. **Entrepreneurship courses:** The names and content of the ones you took, but more importantly, what you liked best about them. Employers in entrepreneurial companies will want to know whether seizing opportunities and embracing unknowns fearlessly is in your blood. If that's what turned you on about the classes, be sure to explain how that resonates with you.

6. **Failures:** Everyone wants to know about times that you have failed. But, in a startup entrepreneurial company, this isn't only about showing what you learned from the experience, rather trial and error is the way of life. So if you are not comfortable admitting that you failed, it is a very dangerous sign. Defensiveness, information hoarding, and hiding bad news can kill a little company. Know why this question is being asked and be honest.

7. **Active engagement in entrepreneur contests:** It doesn't matter whether you won or lost, but did you come up with an idea, hone it with a mentor, learn to pitch it, and advance it to some degree? If so, just the experience itself will be of interest to a startup manager. Explaining how this formed your view about what you want out of your job and career will really seal the deal.

8. **Personal connection to entrepreneurs:** Having a close relationship with people who are entrepreneurs or who work in startups is a plus because you will come into the organization knowing some critical basics, for example, filling voids is the main job of everyone in the company, and what is printed on your business card is irrelevant.

9. **Strive to inspire—your main competitor is yourself:** Employees who constantly seek to outdo their own performance are the most prized pearls in a startup. Having

standards and pride in your work is fundamental, but considering mediocre the quality of the work you did six months ago is the sign of someone who is striving and looking to optimize themselves.

10. **Problem solving:** Comfort grappling with problems and the capability to solve them is essential. Uncertainty is the norm in startups and entrepreneurial ventures. Having demonstrated prowess and desire to solve problems when the answers are neither known nor obvious, not simply being proficient and efficient at executing tasks will differentiate you among highly qualified candidates.

Four Critical Steps to Tee-Up Your Career as CEO

A wise entrepreneur once told me, "The first CEO is rarely the last CEO." He went on to explain that the skill set required to start a company is very different than the talent set needed to grow and manage a successful business. He also explained that there are natural serial passages through which startups progress, and the leader who starts the ball rolling with a discovery or insight is rarely, if ever, the one who moves it all the way through product development and presides over $1 billion in sales.

If you love startups and want to run them, what should you do? The founders are the people best suited for the very early discovery and proof of concept work. But after that, consummate professional leaders are needed to shepherd the company through each critical juncture. It is almost unheard of for a founder to pass the reins; that is the job of the venture capitalists to make happen.

So how do you T yourself up to a venture capitalist?

Simple—follow the T paradigm (see diagram, below):

1. **Develop extraordinary skill at one critical function.**
   You need to become "untouchable" in this area, which

Breadth of Talent					
Market Research	Business Development	Product Development	Financing & Investor Relations	Sales & Marketing	Manufacturing & Quality

T	Level 1
a	Level 2
l	Level 3
e	
n	Level 4
t	Level 5
	Level 6
D	Level 7
e	Level 8
p	Level 9
t	
h	Level 10

typically flows from your undergraduate and graduate degrees. In order to achieve the required level of expertise, it means spending five to ten or more intense years accumulating in-depth skills, and amassing some high-profile accomplishments. You need to be considered beyond reproach. This is the vertical portion of the T; think of it as a series of blocks that are stacked ten high—you need to check-off every one of those ten-depth boxes.

2. **Identify the other important areas for the business to succeed and line them across the top.** This is the horizontal portion of the T. Show competence (3–5 depth levels) in the most critical horizontal breadth boxes and some level (1–3 depth levels) of experience in as many of the others as possible. Begin to seek out responsibilities within your company and other jobs that will allow you to demonstrate competence at these skills. Getting an MBA in finance and then raising money for a company is one of the things that I did to round out my hardcore medical/R&D

vertical portion of the T. I also became a board member, consummated business development deals, and led joint operating committees between companies, which also helped me expand the horizontal portion.

3. **Position yourself.** See how the experiences you have on the horizontal and vertical portions of the T align with the needs of companies in the sector, and construct curriculum vitae that tells the story of how you can add value. Understand your niche, and seek out opportunities. By the time you have checked all ten boxes in the vertical portion of the T, and five out of eight on the horizontal portion, you will have enough contacts, particularly among investors, to be considered a wise choice.

4. **Audit yourself.** Once you become the second or third CEO, the whole shooting match is now your responsibility. Perform a very critical self-audit. Hire the best people you can find who possess the skills you do not have, which the company needs to be successful. The most critical areas will be in the unchecked boxes on the horizontal portion of the T. Drop the ego and supplement yourself, even in areas you have checked off, which require more depth than you have accumulated. Then, you won't just be the CEO; you'll be a good CEO with more longevity than most.

The T approach continues to work for me.

You're the one who has to manage your own career. Do so by carefully picking what you want to do, once you've seen enough to have an informed view. Then you need to become untouchable at a critical function. Next, you should gain as much experience and competence at the other critical, as well as important, functions as possible. Position and package yourself, leverage your contacts, and then attack.

Let me know how you do.

Five Tips for a Successful Company Meeting

In an early-stage company, the all-hands company meeting is the most important means of communicating. In my experience, it is the best opportunity for management to be assured that important information is highlighted and discussed with employees.

In small companies, managing and teaching managers how to manage is often a low priority. It is especially important, therefore, that the boss communicates frequently with the employees to make sure that the message she wants is delivered.

Here are essential elements to incorporate into company meetings:

1. **Conduct a Management Committee Meeting before the company meeting:** Getting on the same page with your management team is critical before addressing the whole company. Let each manager know that he or she will be speaking for five to ten minutes during the company meeting and give them a chance to tell their peers what they will be discussing. Often, they will engage among themselves about initiatives that cross departmental boundaries. Let them know in advance what you will be covering so that they are not blindsided and so they can make suggestions. The meeting cannot be your monologue; employees want to know that the person to whom they report is respected and given an opportunity to talk.

2. **Prepare:** Think about what you want to say days in advance, especially the over-arching theme, so that you can make everything serve this point. Try to leverage something topical that will appeal broadly, i.e., movies, news items, or sports. Let employees see that you prepared by having notes. This tells them that you are in their service and you respect them enough to want to put on a good

show. Work the room—call on employees to help you finish your thoughts; they love being engaged publicly and having the right answer. Admit when they have thought of something germane that you hadn't—humility is a wonderful thing! The company meeting should exhaust you—it should drain you of emotional energy because one of your main goals is to inspire, energize, and give employees a(nother) reason to believe in you and the company. You should be nervous, and even let the employees know that you are.

3. **Limit it to one hour:** Be complete, but disciplined. Share lots of information since very little in a company is truly confidential. If you want employees to feel engaged, think and act outside the box and fill voids, you must inform them of what is happening throughout the company. You want cross fertilization. Employees can concentrate and stand in place if you stick to an agenda, respect time limits, and entertain them with different speakers and topics. Educate them without being pedantic—give them something that expands their minds and makes them reflect.

4. **Be inspirational:** Much of the content necessarily will be mundane, e.g. enrollment period deadlines for health plan announcements, stock trading windows, need for employees who have not completed mandatory training to do so, employee departures and introductions of new hires, warnings about stealing toilet paper, etc. Also, have honest discussions of business performance—Wall Street perceptions, targets not attained, changes that are required because of lack of performance; all must be discussed. Of course, it is simply a must that good performance should be shared and celebrated. Give awards to employees who went above and beyond, and elaborate on how exactly: their behavior moved the needle, perfectly embodied

certain company values, led to an undiscovered opportunity, or enhanced business performance and morale. Begin and end the meeting with something inspirational or a challenge to employees—tee-it-up at the beginning, allude to it throughout, and bring it home with the punch line at the end.

5. **Break bread afterward:** Immediately following the meeting, provide lunch. The Italian in me prefers pizza but Chinese food works, too! Seeing people interact at the buffet line or making room for others to sit, helping a colleague clean-up a spill, or commenting on the food fosters camaraderie and allows those who would normally not have a reason to interact to speak to each other. Seeing fellow colleagues in a different light reminds everyone that we are humans with the same needs and wants; this serves as a subtle reminder of the value of partnership and support. It also gives them time to discuss the events of the meeting, particularly the inspirational, amongst themselves. Let them have their moment. Little companies are a lot like families; those that eat together stay together.

Take your company meeting seriously and you will see enormous direct and indirect benefits.

What you put into it, employees will take out.

Happiness: The Most Obvious Sign You've Put Yours on the Shelf

They say that money can't buy love. But, can it buy happiness? I think it can.

Eight years ago, I was running a public startup medical company located in Westchester, NY and split my living time between a permanent home in Delaware, where my wife lived and worked, and an apartment in New York City where I spent several nights per week. On top of that, I was traveling outside the area on business approximately 40% of the time. On weekends in the winter, we would stay in the Big Apple apartment. Between Thanksgiving and Christmas, our young niece and nephew visited us.

As the children were exploring the small one-bedroom apartment, the high pitched voice of my ten-year-old nephew called out, "Uncle Joe, why are there only drinks in this refrigerator." I ignored him, hoping that he would move on to something else, but he persisted. "Why are there only drinks in this refrigerator?"

I went over angrily to show him he was wrong and opened the refrigerator, and much to my surprise, he was actually right—on the refrigerator shelves and doors were bottled water, Diet Coke, skim milk, and several bottles of Chardonnay. Wait; there was a tub of Country Crock and a few packets of ketchup. And that's it.

On weekends in the summer, when we are at a beach house together, my nephew is accustomed to seeing a packed refrigerator—several buckets of my finely cut fruit salad that takes me more than two hours to prepare, eggs, bacon, whole milk, butter, jelly, Hershey's syrup, deli sandwich meats, cheese, salad dressing, several varieties of lettuce, meats to be grilled (hot dogs, steak, hamburgers, salmon, scallops), Chinese food leftovers from the night before, wrapped-up pizza, peaches, cherries, cottage cheese, yogurt, and a pie.

He is also used to seeing me happy as I prepare the fruit salad and skewers, grill the meals, make coffee, and chat with his parents and my wife.

In the NY apartment, I was not happy at all. I was working, running on adrenalin, rushing everywhere, and trying to get back down to Delaware to see my wife whenever possible. And my evenings and nights in the apartment were very stressful; either I was packing for an out-of-town trip, preparing slides and printing them for meetings with investors the next day, or completing other work. I would order from the Moonstruck Diner, open a bottle of Chardonnay, turn on the Mets or Knicks, and drink as much as I could to wash the day away, but not so much as to prevent me from working out the next morning at 6 a.m.

The last thing on my mind was what I would eat. The last thing I would do is spend the time to go food shopping during the week.

You are what you eat, and you eat what's in your refrigerator.

When you force yourself to shop for food, to prepare, plan, microwave, preheat an oven, slice, peel, and boil, you give yourself distance from the day. The planning and execution of an enjoyable healthy pursuit brings happiness into your life without you even realizing it. Washing the dishes instead of reading reports or trade journals gives a tired mind room to clear itself, and nerves time to calm, naturally.

The expression, "Keepin' it real," basically sums it up. A life without food in a refrigerator is not a real life. You can sustain an artificial existence temporarily, but you cannot do that for years without losing something. I lost a lot, insidiously—I didn't even realize it was happening. I kept telling myself that this was temporary, that the hurdles and challenges the company was facing would soon be over, that Nirvana was just around the corner. But it wasn't.

Working in startups and entrepreneurial ventures does this to you. The sacrifices add up and take their toll. When there are more challenges than successes, you wrongly equate activity itself as winning. So you do more, whether or not it has any vector sum gain, or is just a frenetic pace of harmonic motion. And then, you don't go food shopping.

If there are only drinks in your refrigerator, you're stuck on this dangerous treadmill. Recognize the signs, take stock of your life, get someone to look at your life from the outside and help you see what is happening. I wish that I had done so.

In the meantime, buy a bottle of Hershey's syrup and put it on the top shelf to remind yourself of what is real.

Conclusion

Selfless caring is a character trait that is predicated on personal responsibility and a moral belief system that holds principles and truth as the highest-order goals. Selfless caring drives you to leave people and circumstances better than you found them. It is a virtually limitless source of energy that fuels tireless preparation and incessant trial and error, and personal reinvention. If you selflessly care, you will, in turn, exhibit additional behaviors that lead to winning strategies and desired outcomes, time after time. The engagement, alignment, inspiration, and motivation that a selflessly caring leader engenders cultivates followership.

Selfless caring is what your mother raised you to do, and to the extent that we are social beings, something that we are naturally inclined to do. But, many have stopped selflessly caring with age. Perhaps, they have bitten the apple from the Tree of Knowledge of Good and Evil, or were victimized for selflessly caring, or did not get ahead as quickly as others who were out for themselves.

I did not grow up in a utopian bubble; I was frequently exposed to and victimized by those who did not selflessly care. In medical school during the first class in which we were in contact with patients, I had an eye-opening experience. We learned how to take histories and perform complete physical examinations, and how to

Selfless Caring
Drives

| Tireless Preparation | Relentless Trial and Error |

Enables

- Accepting the profound responsibility
- Following the golden & platinum rules
- Mentoring and being mentored
- Making difficult decisions

- Setting a great example
- Owning that the fish stinks from the head
- Reinventing yourself
- Taking chances on people and cultivating talent

Leads to

Winning Solution / Desired Outcome

Selfless caring drives tireless preparation and relentless trial and error, which enables critical management and leadership habits that lead to the discovery of the winning solution and desired outcome.

monitor patients. It should have been a great class, but it was not. The eleven other students in my cohort and I would complain to each other all the time about it. At the end of the class, the clinical professor asked us to let him know, candidly, what we thought so that he could make it better for next time. I spoke up first and said that it was wonderful to be with patients, but the course should have been much more about how to treat and manage the common diseases, *in toto*. He asked me for specifics. So I told him that my mother's best friend, Mrs. Kay Curcio (God rest her soul) has severe diabetes and every time I see her, she asks me what have I learned new about diabetes, and every time I tell her, "Nothing!" Oh, I have learned about diabetic retinopathy, and gastroparesis, and I have managed foot ulcers, and been in amputation surgeries, and put patients on insulin and oral hypoglycemics, but I never learned about diabetes from start to finish, rather I was taught about it in a completely fragmentary manner. Further, it seemed to me that diabetes, heart failure, pneumonia, and just a few other diseases will comprise ninety percent of our medical practices, so why not focus on these ten or so diseases and take us through them, start to finish in this class?

The instructor was thinking about what I just said when another student chimed in and said, "Professor, I have no idea what Joseph is talking about. I found this to be the most rewarding and amazing class I have ever taken." She got a higher final grade than I did, although I had higher grades on every test and practical assessments. What did I learn from that experience? Nothing! I still speak my mind—politely, professionally, and intelligently—and people with whom I work, live, and love trust me. As for my colleague who stabbed me in the back, somewhere along the line, she unlearned what her mother taught her.

She is not alone. It seems to me that many, many people who have achieved a great deal have strayed from the selfless caring that was engrained in us during our childhood. That is very sad. It is probably why most employees complain about their managers and leaders, and why people are pleasantly surprised when they find someone in authority who is authentic, trustworthy, and inspirational.

For me, being the kind of person whom my mother wanted me to be is a requirement, not an option. Companies would be wise to hire people who have values, and only put those with sound principles in positions of authority and leadership. Employees notice, especially in the critical and unscripted moments, and when it is very tempting and more expedient to sacrifice principles. It is in these moments that our mettle is tested and we are exposed for who we really are. Don't fail the test.

How about when no one is looking? Sorry, no skimping there, either. When I was in college taking organic chemistry—the class that induces the most anguish in pre-med students—I was presented with an interesting choice. I had studied for the third exam tirelessly, as always, but when I tried to answer a ten-point synthesis question—starting with molecule X, synthesize molecule Y in the most efficient manner and show all intermediaries and by-products—I couldn't because I didn't know the structure of molecule X. So I raised my hand and when the professor came over, I showed him the steps to synthesizing Molecule Y from molecules A, B, and C, but, that I couldn't do it from molecule X because it wasn't in our notes. He said, "It most certainly is." [I could rewrite all the notes on blank paper, that's how well I knew them.] I told him that was not the case. He said to me, "I will sell it to you for three points." I said, "No deal because you didn't teach it." He asked, "You are willing to sacrifice seven points on an organic exam?" I said yes and I handed in my paper. He said to wait while he went back to his notes; he came back to me sheepishly and said, "You are right, I never taught it." He thereupon wrote the structure of molecule X on my paper. I said, "No, write it on the board so everyone can see it." He told me that he would not do that because I was the only one who would have known. So I didn't answer the question and I handed in my paper, knowing that I got 10 points off automatically and the highest I could get would be a ninety percent. When the grades came back, I got an eighty-eight. I missed a two-point question earlier on the test.

I chose to live my life and manage and lead others with the principles that my mother, my father, and my faith taught me. When I fail, I recognize it, make amends, and try again.

Summary of the Major Concepts

1. Selfless Caring is a character trait grounded in holding principles and truth as your highest order goals; taking personal responsibility for outcomes and results, as well as for the overall well-being of those whom you manage; and leaving people and circumstances better than you found them. If you selflessly care, you will prepare tirelessly and keep trying until you arrive at the winning solution and desired outcome.

2. Tireless preparation unearths the optimal solution(s) to problems, and it provides a tremendous amount of data from which creative solutions emerge.

3. Management is a gift and a profound responsibility. Many executives don't feel this way, and it shows. The opportunity to touch the lives of employees and those in their sphere is enormous. Done well, the way you manage can change the course of the careers and lives of employees while augmenting the success of the business. In addition, unwavering loyalty follows.

4. The Golden Rule—treat others the way you want to be treated—is a must in order to garner respect from employees who will be inspired to perform and follow your lead because of your egalitarian thinking and authentic team approach.

5. The Platinum Rule—treat others the way they want to be treated—removes you from your egocentric view of the world, allowing you to manage with great empathy and enabling you to individualize your approach to the situation and the employee. True *followership* is earned by leaders who act like Atticus Finch, who don't think they know someone until they climb into another's skin and walk around in it.

6. Trial and error requires reinventing your approach and yourself as often as it takes to be successful in the operational and employee-management challenges that you face. This requires the humility in order to admit something you did actually failed, and creativity and energy to devise and try new ways.

7. Teaching and mentoring enables employees to achieve their greatest potential. The leader also needs to be taught

and mentored so that he can optimize his approach and learn from his failed attempts.

8. A leader is a VISION-AGER, the one whose job it is to identify a concept, path, direction, course, or strategy that people have not yet accepted, and through force of personality and persuasion obtain their support and alignment. Managers are starting with a group of employees who have subscribed to the vision, and their job is ensure dutiful execution. Effective managing is a proving ground for leadership.

9. Making difficult decisions is the job of the leader; they cannot be delegated, nor can the repercussions be ignored. Communicating the rationale to employees is critical in order for them to have confidence in the direction the manager has taken.

10. Always setting a great example and challenging employees to model your behavior is the best way to create an excellent culture. Employee meetings are essential in reinforcing the values and behaviors that are desired.

11. Never asking others to do that which you wouldn't, and doing things that might be interpreted as "beneath" you, is critical for a leader. Employees find this inspiring and model the behaviors.

12. The leader is the keeper of the company culture and value system. You can delegate many things as a leader and manager, but you cannot delegate culture.

13. The leader must show a high degree of "Caretensity"—a combination of selfless caring, intensity, and perseverance. Caretensity exudes passion, sets a high standard of self and team performance, and communicates an attitude that

screams, "We will not be deterred." Employees follow leaders who demonstrate that they have both the skills and the desire to win, and genuine happiness when their employees win.

14. Employees with a sufficient (but not necessarily "off the charts") level of skill and the right attitude are priceless. Managed and led correctly, they become the heart and soul of the company.

15. Taking chances on people and cultivating talent inspires employees to achieve things that they never thought were possible. It also earns loyalty and pays dividends for a long, long time.

16. All of this means nothing if the business is not successful.

Care Quotient

What is your Care Quotient? Are you Caretensive? How much do you care to be the best contributor, manager, and leader you can be? As we discussed, employees can sense when their manager and leader cares about the right things in the right ways, and when he doesn't. And, they are more likely to align themselves and genuinely follow your lead, as well as forgive some foibles and mistakes, if they sense that you care enough to do a great job for the business, communicate to them, and foster their development.

I suggest that you use the following Care Quotient worksheet to obtain feedback about your leadership skills and areas for improvement. This can be given to employees and peers, as well as your managers, as part of a 360-review process. It can also be used in coaching and in providing leadership training to high-potential employees or with managers and leaders who are not performing at the required level.

CARE QUOTIENT SCORECARD

Please provide feedback on _____ by considering the questions contained in the following six areas, providing appropriate examples, and scoring each segment from 0 to 5 at 0.5 increments with 5.0 being the highest score:

Realize Management is a Gift and a Profound Responsibility

To what extent does _____ demonstrate a genuine sense of appreciation for the privilege of managing and leading his/her department/company, as well as an authentic sense of personal responsibility to positively affect the careers and lives of his/her peers and employees? Provide an example.

Provide score _____ based on the following scale:

1. Views management as a job and is not particularly engaged with employees or views employee interactions as a chore.
2. Occasionally provides feedback that facilitates career and personal advancement.
3. Palpates issues that affect employees professionally or personally and proactively engages.
4. Is very aware of the vibe among employees in the department/company, as well as employees' professional goals, and proactively engages in a positive manner and strives to coach them to reach their goals.
5. By specific proactive actions, not just words, makes employees feel that they are as important to her/him as the objectives of the project and company, and is present and available to employees in good times and bad. Proactively coaches employees to attain personal and professional goals.

Reinvent Yourself, as Often as It Takes

To what extent does _____ demonstrate an ability to try new approaches to solve difficult problems? How readily does _____ acknowledge that the approach being taken is not working? To what extent does _____ consider ideas from others? To what extent has _____ changed his/her way of thinking and interacting with peers and employees with increased experience/exposure to individuals? Provide examples.

Provide score _____ based on the following scale:

1. If it is not in the plan, manual, or SOP's, he/she doesn't do it unless told to do it by managers/superiors.
2. Implements new strategies when it is obvious to all that the current course is not working.
3. Occasionally will accept input from employees that results in new strategies and approaches.
4. Solicits feedback from the team about whether courses of action are working appropriately.
5. Proactively seeks input from employees regarding whether strategies are working, assumes responsibility, and changes his/her approach, as well as the strategy when the plan is not working or the desired outcome is not likely to be achieved.

Take the Time to Teach and Mentor, and to be Taught and Mentored

Does _____ take time to teach and advise employees on how best to perform their jobs, deal with difficult circumstances, and advance their careers? Does _____ seek and accept advice, instruction, and training? Provide examples.

Provide score _____ based on the following scale:

1. Shows no interest in explaining or teaching, rather leaves this up to managers and employees.
2. Will teach new employees rudimentary skills to accomplish the task at hand.
3. Takes time to teach and mentor, if asked.
4. Occasionally senses the need to teach and mentor employees and does so proactively.
5. Enjoys teaching and mentoring employees (new and experienced) and embraces and seeks out professional development opportunities for himself to be taught and mentored. Views him/her self as a coach responsible for assisting staff in attainment of company, professional and personal goals.

Make Difficult Decisions

Does ____ take ownership of problems and challenges? Does ____ make tough decisions, or does he/she wait until the decision is made by others or external factors? Is ____ effective at mobilizing a team to consider the best approaches, and does he/she communicate the rationale for the decisions that are made and provide information as to the outcomes and effectiveness of the selected paths? Provide examples.

Provide score ____ based on the following scale:

1. Defers all decision making to supervisors or external factors.
2. Looks to others (subordinates) to make decisions and saddles them with the responsibility and often blames staff or "finger points" for poor decisions.
3. Is not very decisive, but will make a decision if most, if not all, of the group supports it.
4. Occasionally will make difficult decisions under pressure from others (including staff) to do so, but is not comfortable taking the lead and would rather not.
5. Readily makes difficult decisions after soliciting input from employees and peers, takes responsibility for the difficult decisions he/she makes, communicates his/her rationale, and provides follow-up to employees.

Set a Great Example

To what extent have you modeled ____ actions, behaviors, and approaches? Does ____ try to do the right and considered things, naturally, even when he/she is not in a highly visible situation? If all employees comported themselves the way ____ approaches his/her duties, would the project/company be better off? Provide examples.

Provide score ____ based on the following scale:

1. Is not visible enough to employees to set an example.
2. Does not feel it is his/her job to set an example, rather subscribes to the theory of "Do as I say, not as I do."
3. The example that he sets is not one that, if emulated, would have more than a neutral impact on the desired outcome.

4. Is cognizant of the fact that his/her actions are modeled and occasionally shows the way but not on a consistent basis.

5. Works openly and visibly to challenge employees to follow his/her example; does not expect anyone to do that which he/she wouldn't.

Take Chances on People & Cultivate Talent

To what extent is ____ open-minded and accepting of others trying new things (jobs and projects)? To what extent does he/she encourage employees to move outside their comfort zone? Does ____ provide employees appropriate tools and support to be successful in new endeavors? Provide examples.

Provide score ____ based on the following scale:

1. Relies on experienced employees, only.

2. Allows employees to watch as he does things that others have not yet done.

3. If requested, will give limited additional responsibility to employees with whom he has significant experience.

4. Allows employees who request new challenges enough rope to hang themselves.

5. Proactively challenges employees to go outside themselves and take risks, understanding that mistakes will be made, but views mistakes as learning opportunities; provides employees with the support and resources to be successful; and proactively coaches them as they undertake new challenges.

Cares About the Right Things

What is important to ____? What does his/her actions communicate about what he/she cares about most?

Provide score ____ based on the following scale:

1. Cares about his/her standing in the company and is unafraid to sacrifice subordinates and peers to advance himself/herself; viewed by subordinates as driven by self-serving goals.

2. Cares more about performance of the company relative to meeting compensation targets and goals than principles; has an "ends justifies the means" approach; does not appreciate the correlation between employee satisfaction/engagement and company results.

3. Cares about employees only to the extent that they contribute to achieving business targets; has a "what have you done for me lately" approach; can be viewed as uninterested unless the issue has immediate bearing on his/her agenda.

4. Though appropriately puts business goals first, understands that at times forces beyond anyone's control can get in the way; makes an effort (although not consistently) to care about employee's goals.

5. Genuinely cares about advancing the careers and lives of the members of the team while achieving business success, together; understands that (a) employee engagement and satisfaction are directly correlated to bottom line results, and (b) caring about team members (subordinates) is a key component of employee engagement.

TOTAL SCORE: _____

The Care Quotient is the total score divided by 0.25. Scores greater than 112 mean that the leader exhibits Caretensity. Any individual behavior scored below 4, even if the Care Quotient exceeds 112, suggests the need for additional training/coaching. For individuals who are not inclined to be Caretensive, significant training is required, or leadership positions may not be appropriate.

126–140   **Uber-Caretensive**

112–126   **Caretensive**

98–112   **Inclined to be Caretensive**

< 98   **Not inclined to be Caretensive**

It Must Serve the Business

This book is not a manual on how to be a nice guy. Several employees rightfully commented that I was tough on them and on others. (As an aside, I was tougher on myself than I ever was on any employee or consultant, and I think that is one of the reasons that they responded.) The point of this book is that selfless caring is great for business; it is also great for all of the stakeholders. If your caring does not serve the business, the employees are not helped. Positive reinforcement does not buy their groceries, and teaching them does not pay for their utilities. No, the business needs to perform for the good of everyone.

I always believed that for as long as someone was paying my salary, no matter how underpaid I may have felt, it was my job to give the company 100% to make it successful. I also believe that I need to earn my job every day as measured by whether the business was enhanced because of my efforts. I once made that statement at a company meeting and several employees let me know privately that they did not like that sentiment, that their performance was judged daily. No warm words from me over that—I told them that all of us need to prove why we should be allowed in the place tomorrow. I told them that I even feel that I need to earn Adele's love every day. They did not like that, either—love is supposed to be understanding. Maybe.

The business is served best by employees who are aligned and who follow your lead. Therefore, it is your job to stoke their passion and give them reasons to believe and give it all they have. Hiring, training, and managing is an investment of great time and money. The most profitable companies do this well and have a motivated, energized, and aligned staff. It is all about the results.

In 1995, I was President and COO of Anthra Pharmaceuticals. We hired a regulatory professional—since I am very experienced in this phase of the business, we did not need someone senior, but we did need someone with a solid foundation. We hired Tim Urschel, who, like me, had worked at a CRO (contract research organization), so we knew he would have a firm footing. Tim is a very quiet person who preferred to listen rather than speak and he was quite timid, back then. I would constantly challenge him to have more confidence in his point of view and to present alternatives as well as a recommended course of action, rather than being afraid to propose solutions he devised. Why should he look to me to come up with all of the plans when he was closer to the action?

Tim, Denise, Al, and I did some great things, including obtaining approval of a bladder cancer drug (in a very dramatic fashion) that has helped a lot of people. I hadn't spoken to Tim for sixteen years when I asked him to comment about caring in business:

As I reflect back on my days at Anthra and more specifically my relationship with you as my Supervisor, I must say of all the Supervisors I have had over the years, you were the epitome of a true mentor and genuine in every respect—no false motives, or facades. What was very clear from day one was your deep belief in the goodness of people and the desire to, in whatever way you could, help them to better themselves in a way that was gentle, supportive, and caring. I came to Anthra after having worked for a CRO that had grown enormously to become ＿＿＿ and lost the close camaraderie among employees of the organization from when I first started. It became a company where your value was only measured in the number of billable hours you generated and nothing else really mattered. Having come from mainly just working on INDs/CTAs and only bits and pieces of NDAs, you provided me the opportunity for many firsts in my career.

It was my first opportunity of really working on putting together the submission of a complete NDA working with a great team (Denise, Al, Tazewell, Auerbachs, Theresa, and Janice) that proved to be invaluable to my career. In addition, I was afforded the opportunity of managing the process through direct interaction with the

FDA project manager, and at times interacting with the medical reviewer _____. It is rare, as I would later find out, that an Assoc. Director would be left to communicate with the FDA project manager and at times other members of the FDA review team without senior management in the room. You also afforded me the opportunity to continue to gain more broad-based experience in my role in Quality Assurance, including hosting my first FDA GCP inspection at the Anthra Office and going out with Al, his staff (Nancy Murray), and consultants to enhance my GMP auditing skills.

You were a tremendous influence in building my confidence that I could do the job at hand and gently bringing me out of my "shell." I previously was unfortunately the victim of a Supervisor who managed through intimidation prior to coming to Anthra, so I was always afraid of not doing the right thing exactly to expectations of my management and fearful of making mistakes. They also spoon-fed their direct reports only giving them the information they needed to do the immediate task at hand without giving them the big picture. You provided the materials to build the path to get the job done, without actually building the path but by letting me, on my own, build the path—be it setting up regulatory archives, the audit plan/program for the phase 3 trial, etc. Most importantly you were able to manage and engage staff, so that the fear of failure would not be viewed negatively, but as a learning experience from which to draw and grow upon.

I distinctly remember in preparations for the ODAC meeting you were trying to get together the team of experts (KOLs) to block off days for preparation and attendance at the ODAC. In my communications with the FDA project manager around possible dates of when our NDA would be discussed before ODAC you were certain it would be the first day of the ODAC meeting, and planned accordingly around that day. Although I tried to communicate that we had no control over which day we would ultimately be scheduled for, you were certain it would be the first day. However, when we received word that it would be on the agenda for the second day of the ODAC meeting, I knew you would not be pleased. I remember driving over from Carnegie Center to the new office space by Princeton Junction Station that we had moved into, fearing what you would say, knowing that the stress level going into the preparation for ODAC amongst other things was beyond comprehension. However, upon relaying the information it was like a calm came over the room. Essentially you told me we would work through it, and it was at this moment that I truly admired you for your support, acknowledging the stress level of trying to prepare for the penultimate meeting that would essentially determine the future of the company, but you were able to be supportive and immediately we started revising timelines and plans for rehearsals, etc. for the ODAC meeting.

I also remember standing outside of the hotel after the first disastrous ODAC meeting was held and discussing what had just happen and thinking, "Wow, this guy just had a major blow to his career, yet he takes the time to talk with his staff sharing his thoughts even though at that point you had no clear answers on how to proceed. Most Senior Management would have disappeared to closet themselves under such circumstances. You also somehow remained positive that something could be done in the face of Mt. Everest being placed in front of us. I just remember thinking 'Joseph is superhuman, knows how to hold it together,' when the rest of us were pretty dismal and upset after the meeting. (Yes, you may have crashed later in privacy, but you demonstrated true leadership that day).

Last but not least, when the FDA NDA approval letter came with my name on it, it just confirmed for me I had contributed and played a significant role in the NDA submission, and to this day that is the only NDA approval letter with my name on it, even though I have been Regulatory Lead on a number of drug products that went to NDA in other companies. It is a regulatory professional's dream to have an NDA approval letter with their name on it, and to be able to have accomplished that so early in my career because you made it possible, for this I will always be grateful. This is a prime example of selfless caring and mentoring. Needless to say, in my experience in many pharmaceutical organizations it is the VP- Regulatory, Senior Management, or President's name that goes on all FDA NDA cover letters, etc., and therefore it is their name that appears on the NDA approval letter.

I have had Supervisors who manage by intimidation with what we managers termed "shark attacks." This manager would out of the blue burst into your office and start throwing questions at you without context, to the point where I would have to ask "which project are you referring to?", or total hands-off approach and can't be bothered to mentor/support their subordinates, or they are merely concerned about their next career move to advancement under which you are measured in their eyes only by, "what did you do for me today." The end result unfortunately is that their subordinates get frustrated and eventually leave. The vast majority of my supervisors are somewhere in between my experiences at _____ and _____ and then those similar to yourself. It is unfortunately a rare breed that does the selfless caring.

The reason I pushed so hard for our drug to be on the ODAC agenda on the first day was because our experts told me that they would not be available on day two; rather they would be in San Diego at the American Urologic Association meeting. When the FDA did not listen to us and scheduled our session for day two, I knew what it meant, and it wasn't good at all. But, those were the facts and we had to deal with them, and we did. I distinctly remember deciding to have Tim submit all correspondence to the FDA—he put my name on a letter he drafted for an IND amendment that we were making; when I edited it, I put his name in place of mine. It is not that I had an approval letter with my name on it already, which was the case with Leela and the Expedited Review Application; no, I wanted Tim to feel valued, to break through his self-doubt, to have that experience for his career, and to feel confident that I trusted him. It clearly empowered and energized him to do a great job. Business served.

Final Thoughts

If you want to be a leader who will be followed and trusted, one who will lead teams to achieving great business success, and who will experience the extreme satisfaction of positively affecting the careers and personal lives of your employees, you need to practice the values that your mother taught you. From those old fashioned values come many other critical behaviors that will serve you well as a manager and equally important, as a human being.

I hope that the examples presented and candid contributions from employees effectively communicate the power of selfless caring to you, and that you can apply selfless caring with excellent results in your career and life.

Please tell me what you think by tweeting me @josephgulfo, or emailing jvgulfo@josephgulfo.com.

ACKNOWLEDGMENTS

There are many people who made significant contributions to the preparation of this book, many who co-lived the stories and experiences about which I have written, and many who made me the person that I am today. I will try to thank them now.

Adele. To me, there is no more wonderful word in the English language than "Adele."

My brother, Vincent, who taught me what it means to be a leader. And, his girls—Mary, Katie, Laura, and Michelle... interacting with them now as adults is a real treasure that I cherish.

My parents (Betty and Vincent), and sisters (Mary and Liz, and their children John Michael, Christopher, Emily, and Natalie), and Godparents (Joseph and Marie Clementi), and cousin (Michael Clementi), and his family (Andrea, Hailey, and Sara). Adele's family, who provided great support to Adele, and encouraged me—Felix, Adelaide, Tom, Lisa, Donna, Elaine, Michael, Rob, John, Devon, Robby, and JenJen. The pictures in which I look my best are those with Jennifer by my side.

My editor and publishing consultant, Debby Englander, and public relations expert, Sheena Tahilramani.

Professional colleagues and friends from whom I learned a great deal and whose approaches I modeled—Bob Maguire, Aileen

Ryan, Bob McCormack, George Ebright (deceased), Michael Walker, and Kirk Maslin (deceased). Professional colleagues with whom I worked shoulder-to-shoulder and without whom the achievements discussed herein would not have been possible— Dina Gutkowicz-Krusin, Nyq Kabalev, Michael Greenebaum, Jeff Wallace, Claudia Beqaj, Mrinalini Roy, Alexei Smirnov, Alex Tereshonkova, Alla Teresh, Gabe Cruz, Jenna Glauda, Vivian Yost, Diana Garcia-Redruello, Denise Webber, Al Maroli, Jean Mantuano, Mervyn Israel, Bob Humphries, Al Thunberg, Tazewell Wilson, Jack McGrann, Tim Urschel, Janice Pruch, and Dieter Enders.

Friends that I made along the way—Paul Weiss, Dalton Chandler, Greg Chodaczek, Bob Lippert, Marcella Kollman-Hemmerich, Jim Snipes, Beth Roberts, Glenn Burlingame, John Prior, Mark Heller, Stephanie Philbin, Faith Charles, Dave Fox, Chris Yochim, Sara Demy, Gib Dunham, and Denise Verzella.

Patients who trusted me to take care of them and their families, and students who enrolled in my classes.

Teachers with great patience, ability, and passion—Al Klainer, Norman Lasker, Charles Shioleno, Glen Mogan, Dennis Quinlan, Gary Weine, Gary Gerstein, Saad Habba, Carroll Rawn, Pete Stamer, Roberta Moldow, Jane Ko, Andy Rosman, Chris Capuano, Bill Smith, Paul Ward, Frances Kramer, and Br. Michael Dwyer (deceased). Julie Kantor, who, along with Vivian, taught me how to be a better manager and leader.

Priests who inspired me in The Way—Robert Sheeran, Ed Cuiba, Anthony Randazzo, Bob Stagg, Joseph Nealon (deceased), and Ed Duffy (deceased).

ABOUT THE AUTHOR

Joseph Gulfo, MD, MBA, is Executive Director of the Rothman Institute of Innovation and Entrepreneurship at Fairleigh Dickinson University, and a Visiting Scholar at the Mercatus Center of George Mason University. He is passionate about removing obstacles to breakthrough innovation, managing start-up companies, cultivating young managers, and developing products that can make a huge difference in the lives of patients and individuals. He also teaches graduate cancer biology, business and entrepreneurship classes, and maintains an educational cancer biology blog.

With more than 25 years of experience in the biopharma and medtech industries, he has been called on to testify in front of Congress on issues including national Right to Try legislation and "Connecting Patients to New and Potential Life Saving Treatments." His work has been published in the Wall Street Journal, Forbes, CNBC, US News & World Report, Fast Company, Inc., and other national publications. He is also the author of *Innovation Breakdown: How the FDA and Wall Street Cripple Medical Advances*. He received his MD from University of Medicine and Dentistry of New Jersey, and his MBA from Seton Hall University. He lives in New York, NY.